DISCARD

CHILD DEV.
LB   Brown, Mary E.
1027   The integrated day in
.B7793   the primary school.
1969

The integrated day in the primary school

The integrated day in the primary school

Mary Brown
and
Norman Precious
Headmistress Church Hill Infant School
and
Headmaster Church Hill Junior School
Thurmaston Leicestershire

Agathon Press, Inc.

Originally published in England by Ward Lock Educational Co. Ltd.
© 1968 by M. E. Brown and G. N. Precious

U.S. edition © 1969 by
Agathon Press, Inc.
150 Fifth Avenue, New York, N. Y. 10011

SBN 87586-017-6

Library of Congress Catalog Card Number: 77-99525

Printed in the United States

Contents

Foreword by L. G. W. Sealey 7
Introduction 9
1 Development of the integrated day 11
2 The school environment 15
3 The teacher 25
4 The child 36
5 The new adventure – the infant school 43
6 Continuity – the junior school 67
7 A quintet 80
8 Overcoming difficulties 121
9 Postscript 132
Appendix A The Leicestershire scene 136
Appendix B Suggested equipment and materials 140
Bibliography 151
Index 157

To the children of Thurmaston

Foreword

One Saturday morning, some ten years ago, a small group of us met in a classroom of the old building of Thurmaston Junior School on the outskirts of the City of Leicester. Armed with tools and boundless energy, we had come together to create the learning environment for the first 'integrated day' in a Leicestershire junior school. The day seemed long and hard and the job was not completed. Nevertheless, on the Monday following, a group of slightly bewildered but excited children took over the room. The experiment had begun.

The present book, by the same headmaster of the school and his colleague who is the headmistress of the associated infant school, describes the ways in which the term 'integrated day' has now been interpreted in their schools. The account is a fascinating one, not theoretical and idealistic, but firmly rooted in real experiences and honest endeavour.

Children in primary schools are perhaps our most precious heritage. Their time is very special in the sense that the stages of development through which they pass do not recur. We cannot afford to ignore any changes in patterns of school experiences that promise increased realization of the many kinds of potential with which these children, in varying degrees, are endowed.

I hope that very many practising teachers, and students in colleges of education, will read this book and find in it a wealth of ideas to spark off their own thinking and action.

December 1967

Leonard Sealey
North Buckinghamshire College of Education
Bletchley Park, Bletchley.

Introduction

'The integrated day' is a term now widely used in education.

When asked to write a book about 'the integrated day', we were aware that many teachers would already have their own interpretation of this way of working. This factual account of what takes place in our schools is our own particular interpretation. The book is written to be helpful to teachers but also to parents who are often puzzled by 'new methods' of education.

The title seems hardly adequate to describe the way children in our school spend their day, for here there is an integration of the child's experience and learning which may be within the framework of an 'integrated week'; and even within the whole of the child's life in primary education – 'an integrated six years'.

The infant school and junior school are on the same campus but are accommodated in separate buildings. There are no barriers between the schools and it is our intention that they should function as one, with a common philosophy, shared amenities and interests.

The schools stand on a hill on the edge of an industrial conurbation and overlook the countryside to the west.

May, 1968.

Mary Brown
Norman Precious

CHAPTER ONE

Development of the integrated day

It is only just over 150 years ago that some seven-year-old children were working a sixteen-hour day and for some time after the Education Act of 1870, which introduced compulsory State education, the scope of the schools was very limited. Education based on mechanical proficiency, the obedience and passivity of the pupil and verbal instruction by the teacher was the general rule. Most teachers were instructors and ruled by fear. They were paid according to the number of attendances and the children's success in examination results. During the tragedy and chaos of the Second World War, evacuation brought to light the terrible poverty in certain areas and conscription revealed a great deal of illiteracy. Butler's 1944 Education Act was the result of the public outcry for the situation to be improved and this Act stressed that education should be made available to fit the requirements of each and every child and it should be an education suitable for his age, aptitude and ability.

Through educational, psychological and physiological research attention was gradually being drawn to the fact that learning is a result of both maturation and experience. The findings of Piaget, the Swiss psychologist, in particular stressed the clearly defined sequential stages in the development of 'concepts'. These stages although sequential are tied closely to each individual child's own experience and maturational level. As these thoughts filtered through to the teachers of young children, they began to look at the children as individuals and to doubt the validity of the teaching methods they were using. Many of them had already started experiments to find more suitable ways of encouraging individual learning. At first, the emphasis continued to be laid on the 'three Rs' and although the methods used were described as 'activity methods', their main and almost exclusive goal was to develop the child's academic ability. Today, educational philosophy asks for attention to be given to the complete development of the child as expressed by Edna Mellor in *Education through Experience in the Infant School Years*:

> My philosophy of education is concerned with the whole child – his physical, mental and spiritual growth; his feelings, attitudes and relationships; his character and personality. It is concerned with him as an individual having certain innate tendencies, potentialities and traits, and also with him as a member of society having certain rights and privileges, duties and responsibilities.

The word 'activity' was misunderstood by certain sections of society who thought of it purely in terms of physical activity and this misinterpretation sadly delayed progress in the use of the activity method. It was not until the activity of the mind and the emotions was included in the true definition that it was more widely adopted. The teacher's role as an instructor decreased and the activities widened to include all aspects of development. As the size of classes decreased, schools felt more able to experiment with new and progressive ideas. Experiments in non-streaming and vertical grouping were being carried out and it seemed that the right circumstances for the integrated day to develop were more naturally achieved in a class which was vertically grouped.

Architects' designs were influenced by the new ideas and there was a remarkable change in the planning of school buildings. They were planned as places where children could live and work together. There was more space and light in the schools and for the first time real concern that the child's environment should be aesthetically pleasing.

As the children worked in this new atmosphere, the teachers began to see the practical proof of the value of this new climate in education. They observed the child's excitement in discovery and learning and his willingness to persevere with even an arduous task if he were personally involved. The teachers were surprised by the natural creativity of the children when they were allowed freedom of expression. Subjects and interests soon became integrated quite naturally as children worked out their individual ideas. The school day was gradually being determined by the interests and needs of children and indeed becoming a facsimile of what we now term 'the integrated day'.

The integrated day could be described as a school day which is combined into a whole and has the minimum of timetabling. Within this day there is time and opportunity in a planned educative environment for the social, intellectual, emotional, physical and aesthetic growth of the child at his own rate of development. Our definition extends this day to encompass the whole life of the child during the six years of primary education.

The natural flow of activity, imagination, language, thought and learning which is in itself a continuous process is not interrupted by artificial breaks such as the conventional playtime or subject barriers. The child is encouraged to commit himself completely to the work in hand which he has chosen. The child also has the time to pursue something in depth even though it may take several days. As he works, problems common to various subjects will arise but within the integrated framework he can make easy transition between any areas of learning.

As the child works, he is involved with learning as an integrated unit coping perhaps with a foray into maths, science, geography, art or English in a short space of time, through the use of books, material and equipment which may lead him into various channels. Subject barriers are extraneous. No limit is set to the exploration involved, which may go off at any tangent into any sphere of learning.

Different subjects are also cemented by the free use of language. If we take for example any one term such as 'three dimensional', this is used in science, maths, English, construction or art and the child may have experience of and explore 3D within a framework where they are all interwoven and almost indistinguishable one from the other or as part of a differentiated subject.

In a school where the integrated day is in practice, the environment is all-important. It must be so well planned, challenging, interesting and attractive that the child wants to become involved with the materials, wants to satisfy his curiosity and to learn. The challenge of the environment must of course be within reach of the child and the provisions not be so complicated that they cause confusion. The day starts as soon as the child arrives. As he works with the material and people around him, his interest is aroused. He begins to think, reason and formulate his ideas in words. He becomes involved with deeper and wider learning. Each day there is opportunity for him to learn and communicate intellectually, physically and artistically in the medium of his choice. Each child will be able to work at his own rate and depth and usually for as long as he likes.

In such a classroom, children can work out their relationships with each other and come to terms with their own impulses. There is legitimate outlet for feelings of insecurity, hate, fear, aggression and love in dramatic, imaginative, social and creative spheres. Certain children need this as therapy and to help them towards emotional and social adjustments. The child must feel fairly secure within himself and with the social and physical world around him or he will be prevented from becoming completely absorbed in his activities and unable to express himself freely. Within each day there is provision for the natural rhythm of each child where there are times of deep concentration followed by less involved work or relaxation. For the child to have the freedom to choose an activity, to be alone or with a group is an essential feature of this environment. The element of choice allows for the needs of the child and will encourage spontaneous personal involvement and concentration to the exclusion of external activities and noise.

The school is an integrated social unit with all types of children learning to live and work together. Ideally they are free to use the whole of the school and are not strictly confined to one teacher in one room. There must be mutual understanding and respect between the teacher and the child. The teacher's role is that of an adviser and guide. She will often become an active participant and will use opportunities to stimulate further discovery, deeper study, vivid imaginative and creative ideas and thought.

The priorities are closely related to the principles involved in sociology in that they are deeply concerned with the needs of the individual and his obligations to the group of which he is a member. Many schools are already working this way and have gone through a steady and continual evolution to reach this or a similar point of arrival.

CHAPTER TWO

The school environment

In our description of the ideal environment for the integrated day, the amenities are a mixture of imagination and reality. Many of these will perhaps never be incorporated in the planning of schools but this is an idea of the Utopian environment which would be in keeping with the philosophy presented in this book.

The school buildings are set in well planned grounds, have an open aspect and easy access from all directions. There are shrubberies, rose trees and flower beds, as well as paved and grassed areas. The playground is not just a rectangle of asphalt but is of irregular shape, has seats, walls and steps and there are secluded patios where people can wander. The playing fields are marked out with the various types of pitches and in the far corner is a pavilion. In the grounds there is a covered swimming pool which is used by even the youngest children. There is a grassed mound which on one side is shaped into a terraced slope to form an amphitheatre and on the other has steps, tunnels, caves, hollows and many other exciting provisions for exploration and adventure. A plot of land is set aside to be used by the children for gardening activities. Here there is a greenhouse, cold frames and a potting shed and a farming area. The head of the school has persuaded the groundsmen to leave a part of the grounds to grow wild and has 'helped nature' by planting a variety of trees, bushes and wild flowers. This is designed to attract birds, butterflies, animals and insects for the children's continuous observation and is a vital centre for much of the school's activity. One of the features is a dew pond where pond life abounds. Although the children make visits to parks and countryside by coach, this natural area at the school is immediately accessible for an individual child or a small group and they are able to make observations of the changing phenomena in the same situation day by day.

The school itself is light and airy and is decorated in carefully chosen colours, with some walls featured in designed wall paper or brightly coloured hessian panels. Natural wood, stonework and brick are all utilized in the fabric of the building. Certain other fabrics used in the school have been carefully chosen and matched to the décor The décor has been worked out to be aesthetically pleasing but it is obvious that it has always been borne in mind that this is primarily a child's environment. To help the children in their acceptance and appreciation of a high standard of creative work, original works of art including paintings, sculptures, pottery and tapestries are an integral part of the environment.

The floors throughout the school are covered with wooden blocks, thermoplastic tiles or carpet according to the use of the area. Certain educational aspects are incorporated here. As one example, the thermoplastic tiling is in geometric shapes, or the environment is exploited to draw children's attention to scientific principles and natural phenomena. Mirrors are skilfully placed to show repeated images, to function as periscopes or to see round a corner, prisms angled to throw spectrum colours from the sun, mobiles suspended in a current of air. There are fountains and tanks of fish and terrapins.

The main foyer is an attractive entrance to the school and large enough to serve as an area where exhibitions can be mounted as well as place where children can work. This leads to the library area on one side and to the main hall on the other and can be incorporated as part of the main hall when necessary. Storerooms for PE apparatus, music equipment and spare furniture are at the side of the hall and have a door to the outside.

The teaching spaces divided from each other by movable walls have access on to outside terraces and to a separate working area fitted with sinks and benches. Each class has lavatory and cloakroom accommodation as well as a storeroom. Raised platforms and steps are an architectural feature and extensive use is made of different levels in the classrooms and around the school.

There is a projection room which can be completely blacked out, a music room, a languages room, a club room and several comfortable carpeted rooms to which the children can withdraw. The clay room has a stone floor which can be easily hosed down together with a kiln so that clay models of the older children can be fired. A plant house, an animal house and a place for weather observation would all exist in the ideal building. The large comfortable staffroom

A general view of an infant classroom with the clay table in the foreground and a variety of activities in progress.

An infant group at work on some mathematical activities with another group using the easels in the painting corner in the background.

An infant boy at work on a mathematical construction.

is situated away from the noisier parts of the school, but is not so inaccessible that it is too far away from the teaching areas. A medical room, the headteacher's room, a secretary's office and spacious storerooms are all part of the administrative block.

In the grounds surrounded by trees and bushes is a rough adventure playground where children can be completely free to explore, adventure and experience with hardly any bounds to the possibilities of its use. It includes a barren area where the children may build and dig, construct Indian encampments, caves or whatever they wish and a Nissen hut where they can enjoy the same sort of freedom under cover.

The school is also in use as a community college and although most of the activities take place after school, there is a room available for daytime classes, or it can be used as a lounge or common room for the people from the community at all times and is often in use by groups of parents. This has separate access. The kitchen and dining accommodation for school meals is a separate entity with connecting doors to the main school.

These ideal conditions are not essential to the successful practice of the integrated day. Old school buildings can be modified and adapted to fit in with newer methods of education. These often have a warm friendly atmosphere which in a new building takes time to develop.

The school is part of the community in which the children live, but when they go to school for the first time, they are starting life in an environment which is different from home and is strange and new to them. However carefully planned this environment may be, it is still, in comparison with home, an artificial situation. Here, as the child meets a wider group of peers and adults than before and as he uses the materials in the school environment, his development and growth is encouraged and continues.

The child is given the freedom to choose the things with which he wants to become involved and this can be achieved more easily where there is no parcelling out of time or directing of groups of children to different activities. The spotlight has, in effect, shifted from the activities or subjects, to the child and his particular interests. Children just entering school will need time to get used to the new situation. If they join an existing group of children, a vertical group for example, they adjust easily and quickly. If however the class is a whole group of reception children, more care must be taken to see that the amount and variety of materials is not so great that the child is overwhelmed by the formidable task of 'choosing'. Too wide a choice would seem paradoxically to be almost as limiting as too little and many teachers feel the need to withdraw certain things from the classroom and reintroduce them at what seems a more appropriate moment.

As the children arrive at school first thing in the morning, they come straight in and quite naturally start to do things. Many will be continuing an activity from the day before. Some will be attracted by a stimulating piece of equipment in maths or science. Some will become immediately involved with creative expression in various media. Others will go straight to the section for domestic or dramatic play, some to the reading area or any of the other activities available in the room and some will just chat with a friend. This is the start of the day. For this to happen, the materials and apparatus must be readily available and within easy reach. The children need to feel responsible for organizing and using their own materials and clearing up adequately and well. Even the young children are capable of this discipline and it is a very necessary part of a well run classroom.

Children engaged in activity use their initiative and are challenged to work, to think, to communicate and are given time to follow what is important to them in their own way and at their own speed. With all this in mind, division of the day by timetabling is now unnecessary and is an interruption in the child's natural flow of interest.

The teacher watches what is happening as the children explore the materials. She will see evidence of the child's immediate interests and needs, will see him meeting and solving problems and it is round these ideas that she makes her plans. The teacher must not be too obtrusive and yet must be aware of what is happening in the room. The children must be able to feel her support when necessary and the room needs to be so arranged that she can see where and when her help is needed. At times, the child may feel the need to withdraw from the teacher or from other members of the class. Some children often prefer to work in bounded areas and these are things to be taken into account when planning the room. Careful consideration must be given to the physical arrangement of the environment. Each classroom varies considerably in shape and size and in the actual arrangement of furniture lies much of the success or failure of the room. The classroom is divided into areas for various activities. Obvious essentials are that the children

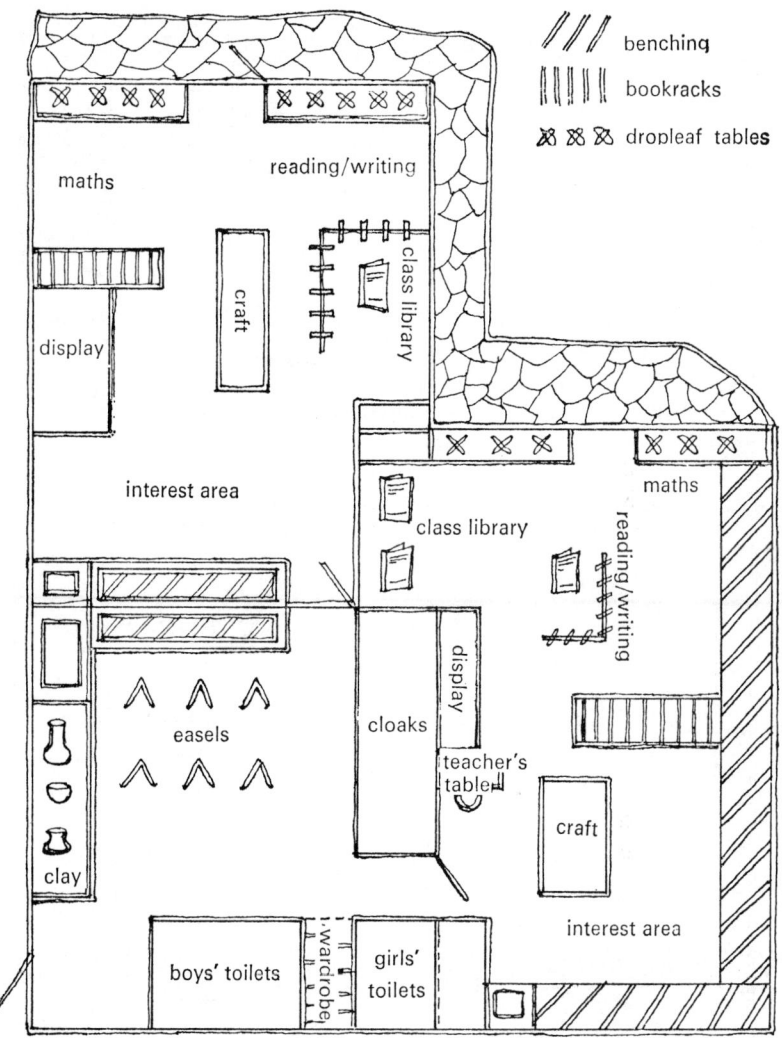

On this and the next page are two arrangements of rooms suitable for infant and junior age children. These are only suggestions and incorporate some of the ideas expressed in the text. It should also be remembered that these arrangements must be flexible and capable of frequent adaption to the prevailing needs of the children.

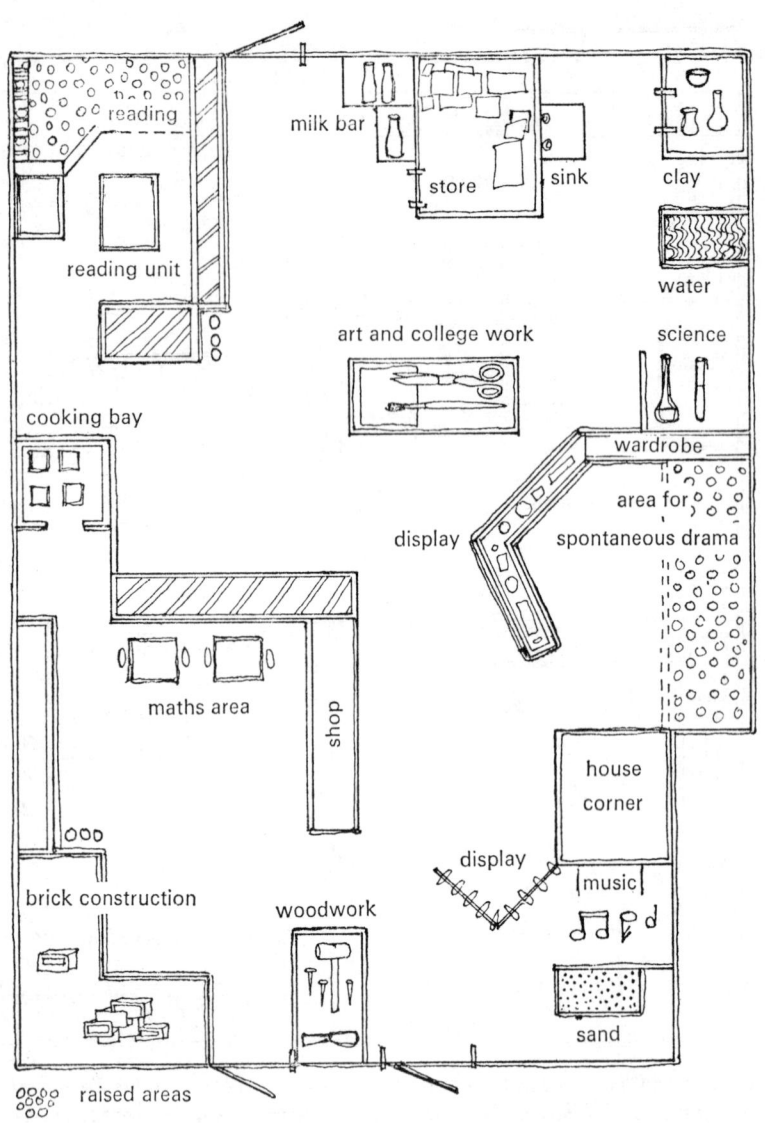

should be able to pursue the noisier activities without disturbing the rest of the group, and that painting and water play should be as near as possible to sink facilities. Construction work is safer in a part of the room where the buildings will not be continually knocked down by passers by. The reading and writing area will need plenty of light and the domestic corner access to an outside area if possible.

It is a good idea to draw the room to scale on graph paper. Each piece of furniture can then be drawn to scale and cut out so that it is possible to arrange the activity or subject areas in miniature and easily find what seems to be the most advantageous arrangement. Definite places will need to be devised for the storage of the various types of material and apparatus. It must be remembered however that where the day is a mêlée of activity with no definite dividing line between the various activities, or indeed between the child's range of interest and thought, there must be the freedom for the children to combine materials, to try using them for things other than their original purpose. Blocks for example can be used as weights, or magnets as part of a building and the teacher should be prepared for this integration of materials and apparatus and take this into account when planning the arrangement of her room. Whilst a room needs to be well equipped with purchased apparatus, the children will also need a wealth of other materials for all types of work. These should include the elemental materials of sand, clay, water and wood. A wide variety of man made material including scrap and waste and many things from the natural environment need to be provided, as well as tools and aids of all kinds to use with these materials in order to change them and to experiment with them. The teacher should always be aware of colour, shape and texture when choosing materials. It is important that all this should be classified and kept in order. Fabrics must be kept flat and pressed and clay at the right consistency for use. So that the children do not meet with more frustration than is necessary, tools need to be kept sharpened. There should not be any shortage of supplies. The general appearance of the room needs to be attractive and interesting although it should be remembered that it is a workshop and will inevitably look as if it is well used by children.

Ideally, the furniture in the room should consist of light, movable, stackable tables as well as some additional large working surfaces. The trapezoidal type formica-covered tables are ideal as one type of surface especially as they can be arranged in so many ways.

A variety of arrangements of trapezoidal tables

The book corner and domestic corner need some small occasional tables. Large working surfaces can be provided by using old trestle tables, arranging flat-topped desks together in fours, sixes or eights, and by having tables hinged to the wall for working on or for display areas which can be folded down to make more space available in the room. Still more working space can be made available if the room is equipped with flat-topped desks. Two facing flat-topped desks can be extended by using a tray between them secured by cotton reel 'feet' which fit into the empty inkwells.

Children often prefer to work on the floor and it would be ideal if a satisfactory way could be found to provide opportunity for this. It might be an idea to use various sizes of boxes or platform units for children to assemble their own raised areas. A platform about a foot or eighteen inches from the floor is an excellent working area especially if it has an easily cleaned surface. There is no longer the need for a place to be available for each child. Seating accommodation may include ordinary chairs, benches, window seats, comfortable armchairs, stools, a rocking chair, rugs, carpets and cushions. Sets of open lockers or locker units on castors about 3 feet high and 4 feet

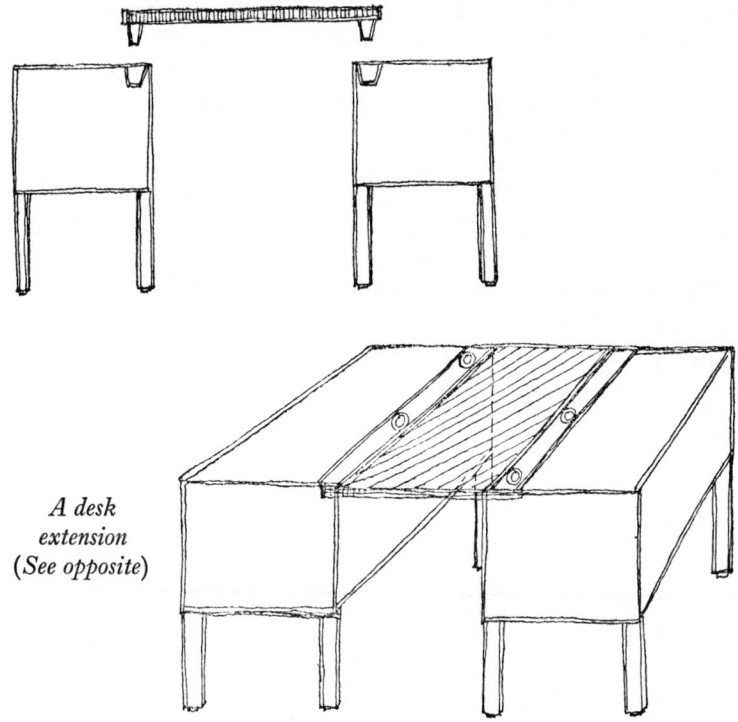

A desk extension (See opposite)

6 inches long with a pegboard back make excellent room dividers, and if these have a section fitted with individual small drawers, each child can have a place to keep his own books and belongings. The Wendy House is a familiar piece of equipment in infant schools but a plentiful supply of three sided screens made in double pegboard which can be assembled for various uses such as shops and houses or as room dividers and display boards seem more useful and adaptable pieces of equipment.

Pinboard areas on the walls at a suitable height for children to use are essential. There will have to be some provision for storing dressing-up clothes, junk materials and bricks, which could be boxes, wire baskets, a 'beanstalk' or low cupboards. A fixed wall blackboard for the children's use, painting easels and trays, baths or tanks to hold clay, wet sand, dry sand, water or other such materials are needed. The polythene tank with a tubular steel stand on castors is ideal for water because of its transparency, but anything can be pressed into service here, from a six-foot tin bath to a rubber dinghy. Book corner standing units, fitments or book trolleys which display books to show the front covers will make them more attractive to children.

Some plans of arrangements have been suggested but each teacher must, by trial and error, plan a room which is suitable to her own particular circumstances. The placing of the large furniture inevitably determines the storage of the apparatus and materials. It would be an impossible task to prepare a comprehensive list of materials needed in the primary school and it would not be expected that the list provided as an appendix to this book would be present in its entirety all at the same time or in any one room but it is offered as a suggestion.

CHAPTER THREE

The teacher

For some people the public image of a teacher has changed little since the beginning of this century. When teachers and classrooms are mentioned, most adults think of a blackboard and chalk, ink and steel nibs, rows of desks, children with their hands up, and the marking and correcting of exercises. The feelings which colour this picture are those associated with sitting in rows, walking in lines, keeping to the left, 'no talking', harsh discipline and the fear of being 'sent out' or 'found out' with the ever-present threat of the cane hovering in the background. In this environment the teacher was usually thought of as an unapproachable instructor and dictator, seldom with any feelings of affection. The change of climate in primary schools means that harsh discipline and strict rules and regulations have been replaced by a friendly, happy, more permissive atmosphere where the code of behaviour is inherent in the school situation.

Teaching is a vocation. It is a profession which is very demanding and even more demanding in the integrated day situation. It is essential that a teacher should have a life outside school which will contribute to her personality and which will preserve her freshness of outlook and influence her work. The most successful teacher functions rather like the champion swimmer who uses fifty per cent effort and fifty per cent relaxation. This fine balance between using the right amount of drive without anxiety has remarkable repercussions in the classroom. Only those who are working in schools because they feel it is worthwhile and satisfying are able to cope with the frequent exhaustion and occasional frustration which is inevitable in the teaching profession. As well as being intelligent and well trained, the teacher needs to be an adjusted, resilient and sympathetic person having a fund of humour and common sense. Teaching could be classed as an art and a science. Perception and creativity are the two essential characteristics possessed by the inspired teacher. She must be sensitive to other people's feelings and attitudes as well as being aware of her own personality, her limitations and capabilities. The teacher who has an inner contentment and freedom from anxiety will find it easier to use tolerance in her dealings with the children. This is the ideal person to work in a primary school, particularly in an integrated day situation.

In a progressive primary school the teacher does not play an authoritarian role but is rather a participant in the living and learning situation in the classroom. She has the final responsibility for making decisions and setting the boundaries between what is acceptable and what is unacceptable in the room; but the discipline of the group is based on mutual respect between the teacher and the child, and between child and child and is gradually assumed as a group responsibility. If the teacher accepts the child and he in return has an affectionate regard for her, he will begin to incorporate the teacher's values and to develop internal personal control. Teachers should understand consciously the difference between 'love' and 'identification' on the part of the child and the importance of encouraging 'identification' to develop. Children are not always virtuous and many teachers have various techniques for maintaining control in the class. If these are based on prohibition and threats, they may do far more harm than is at first realized. Any punishment employed by the teacher is better if directed at 'the act' rather than the child and in any situation should never humiliate the child. At all times the teacher should be aware that with one ill-timed remark she can perhaps damage the *rapport* which she has already established between herself and a child and cause him to withdraw or develop further aggression. The wise teacher uses less harmful ways of imposing the boundaries of behaviour and, carried out with understanding, these will not harm the teacher–child relationship or injure the dignity of the child. Where there is a good relationship, the direct appeal, a look or gesture or a straightforward 'No; that is just not allowed' is sufficient. Sometimes it may be necessary to give the child an explanation of why it isn't allowed. A teacher who can smile at a child who is indulging or about to indulge in bad behaviour, or perhaps move closer to him or show interest in what he is doing, will find that this increased show of affection always seems to bring the required response. The teacher can at any time in the integrated day restructure the situation to dissipate tension if things are not running smoothly. If the teacher can keep the child as free from frustration as possible by stepping in before tension occurs, if she makes sure that the children are well aware of the limits (for boundaries do exist although they are wide ones) then the atmosphere will be relaxed. Briefly, one of the teacher's tasks is to create a relaxed and easy atmosphere based on trust, mutual understanding and respect. Before this can happen, the teacher herself must be happy and secure within the school environment and enjoy the trust, respect and confidence of her colleagues. It is essential for the teacher to recognize the great responsibility for the welfare of the child which she shares with the parents. The child's attitude towards the teacher will be akin to his feelings for his parents and the teacher must be prepared to cope with certain resentments and erroneous judgements on the part of the child because of the emotional overtones associated with his early interactions with his parents. The teacher's voice is one of the most important items of her 'stock-in-trade', not because it must be loud and commanding but because it is in constant use to converse and explain and help.

The teacher is interested in the child's complete development, is aware of his successes and his failures, his disappointments and anxieties. This is only possible if she can establish an intimate personal relationship so that the child will turn naturally to her for help, approval or advice. This relationship, based on mutual respect is essential for the child's success in learning. Alan Frome who writes the foreword to John Holt's book *How Children Fail* talks about the importance of the relationship which exists between the teacher and the child and stresses the need for teachers to learn to see their pupils and to have the sensitivity to build up the intimacy in the teaching–learning situation ideally necessary for intellectual growth. There is, in the integrated day, opportunity for this to occur. The teacher is able to watch the children, discover their individual idiosyncrasies, become aware of their needs and develop a relationship with each child, which, although closely akin to the parent-child relationship in that it is deeply concerned for the child and his well being, is also more objective. The teacher and the child become friends but neither must become a demanding or presumptuous friend. The teacher is the child's partner in this relationship and in turn she learns much from the child. There is a communication in the good teacher–child relationship which is indefinable. They really 'know' each other and can communicate immediately, perhaps with a word, a look or a gesture, or often even without these outward signs. It is all part of this mutual respect, awareness and understanding which develops but cannot be explained precisely. In return the children of course watch the teacher; they note her reactions, test her, learn from her and learn about her. Everything that the teacher does has an effect of some kind. This is a great responsibility for the teacher and almost frightening in its vast implications. Children are astute and they sense quickly whether the teacher is really interested in them and what they are doing. Her participation is essential. The children soon know if she is genuinely interested or just putting on an act to try to encourage them. Respect, trust, confidence, affection and lack of fear are some of the ingredients which go to make up the relationship.

The teacher must be ready to concede that she is not always right. If she assumes a dictatorial attitude and imparts information which the children are expected to accept without question, they will not be encouraged to think critically about anything. They will never develop their own ideas when it is at the cost of rejecting the teacher's ideas. It is important too, that she is not afraid for the children to know that she is a human being and so has weaknesses as well as strengths. The tendency in the past was for the teacher to be afraid to show a 'chink in the armour' and the children were faced with the impossible task of trying to model themselves on this infallible being who had no faults and was never wrong. The teacher will respect the children's rights and opinions and encourage a happy, informal, unhurried atmosphere in the room where the children do not feel worried or overanxious. If the teacher had difficulties in her own childhood, she might find it very difficult to cope tolerantly with similar situations such as aggression, quarrelling, curiosity or pilfering, which arise in the classroom and this can bring disharmony to an otherwise relaxed atmosphere.

The teacher is in charge of the classroom and it is her responsibility to make the environment (well supplied with suitable apparatus and materials) attractive and thought provoking and one in which there is the widest opportunity for the development of the children's creativity and intellectual ability. Through the provision of materials and equipment she can so condition the situation that the children will follow definite leads to specific experiences which she may decide they need.

In organizing a class on activity lines and working an integrated day, the teacher must have real conviction and understanding of the underlying philosophy and have the confidence in herself to carry it out, feel secure in her ability as a teacher, enjoy the thought of the unexpected happening in her room and of the classroom scene changing hour by hour. Her resources for books, equipment and materials may not always be great but her imagination and initiative help to make up for deficiencies. The interests of a teacher are contagious. If she needs and refers to books, has natural gifts or skills or appreciation of the arts, her children will tend to echo these. Above all, if she has enthusiasm and energy her class will be enthusiastic and energetic. To make adjustments and allowances for the forty children in her care is a mammoth task, particularly for the newly qualified teacher or for a teacher who is not experienced in these methods. If she manages not to exert pressure or bully the children into activities, she will find that they will develop interests in the materials provided and some children will bring interests into the classroom from outside. If the right environment is provided and the teacher can be patient, then exciting things will begin to happen.

According to Piaget 'the teacher sees and seizes opportunities for talking to the children. For play to be fully educational, the teacher must be an active participant acting as interpreter and instructor' and to Piaget the main task of the teacher is to help to develop the child's mental processes by aiding growth and understanding, not by giving answers, but by posing questions, helping the children to verbalize and formulate their ideas and thoughts. He stresses that there must be opportunities for the children to question and try to explain what they are doing so that they increase in their ability to classify and organize their thinking. It follows therefore that the teacher must observe the children carefully to ascertain their developmental needs and find ways of meeting them, and she must always be aware of the importance that the 'giving of the right words' will play in any situation. She must also watch and follow the real interests of the children. Children will always be excited and stimulated to work on things that are nearest to their hearts. As they watch, explore, experiment and collect, observe, create, try to solve their own problems, talk about them, work out possible results, try out and criticize the results, they are led on to further exploration and experiment and so the momentum grows.

Whilst the children work, the teacher will encourage them to talk about what they are doing although sometimes their absorption will be too intense to do this. There is a great deal of skill in knowing when to initiate discussion. Through discussion and conversation with individual children where the teacher uses the correct words for things rather than a simplified version, their vocabulary will increase, their speech become a more precise definition of their meaning and their understanding develop. It does not mean that a child understands something just because he can talk well about it but the teacher is aware of the depth of his understanding. The teacher encourages the child to talk through his 'actions' but tries to make the talk more valuable by providing provoking situations. She will join in conversations and provide the necessary words for the children to formulate and extend their ideas. Whilst the teacher is a working member of the group and the emphasis is on children learning rather than the teacher teaching, it is obvious that if she is the right kind of teacher, she will engender interest, enthusiasm and inspiration. At times she may play a waiting game; she will also choose certain moments to step in and extend, help or guide a child, ask a question or suggest that he refer to a certain book for details and information. Some educationists who are not actually teachers often express concern about intervention. A good teacher seems to act intuitively here. She does not always stop to analyse whether it is appropriate for her to interfere at a particular point, but the skill of knowing when to give guidance and when not to interfere, comes with experience and through the knowledge of each particular child. The teacher will however need to assess the development of each child objectively so that she is able to determine the stability of understanding of concepts and so ensure progression. There will always be a few children who will need more help than others and the teacher is able to give them this added attention. The children will need help in various techniques such as the correct use of tools or the mixing of paint; but always in view is the aim to make the child as independent and self reliant as possible and to encourage his maximum mental activity. Quite often, after the child himself has approached for help, he may take time to consider it and eventually perhaps even reject or modify the teacher's idea. In maths or science for instance, it is not our job to show or tell conclusions but to make sure that conditions are at the optimum within the classroom for the child to have experiences through which he will discover his own conclusions. The teacher gives scope to the child to choose and to carry out his own ideas, tries to see what he is attempting, helps as much as possible by the provision of appropriate materials, by asking questions, by discussion and sometimes suggestion but she must also beware of imposing her own ideas on the child to the detriment of his original aim.

The teacher will soon learn to recognize when a child requires a fresh stimulus. Sometimes the interest in a particular activity may be very short lived and the right decision on her part is to let it die. At another time, the child must be helped to work through a difficult patch; for the aim of this way of working is not to make things as easy as possible but that the children should learn to work as well as possible. As a teacher gets to know her children individually, she learns when best to make suggestions which may lead the child into further work on a chosen subject. She will have to work alongside some children and become involved herself, whilst with others, a short discussion, the right question at the right time or the offering of advice or help may suffice. She may help in discussing the manner in which the information can be presented. Sometimes a child may not fully understand the text of a reference book or really understand the idea presented. A problem of this kind may be solved by referring to other books or to other people with more knowledge of the subject. The teacher should not assume the role of being a source of information but encourage children to find things out for themselves. On the other hand, if the teacher does not know, it would be better to be honest and admit it but suggest a way that they could both find out. The right question at the right time will help children over the hurdle of 'what comes next'. A discussion may fire a child's imagination and desire to find out. Assignment cards can be used at certain stages to stimulate an interest and arouse curiosity; they should not reveal the whole story but rather take the child on to the threshold of discovery and leave him with a strong desire to find out more.

During the day, the teacher will be looking for opportunities to make the children more aware of the possibilities of the material in the environment to see how they can exploit the functions of any of the hundreds of ordinary things which surround them every day. As an example, let us take a common object which is regularly brought to school and explore its possibilities – a plastic bottle for liquid detergent. The child could first enjoy squeezing the bottle and expelling the air slowly or quickly and watching the effect on something else, listening to and changing the sound emitted, working out musical rhythms with the expellation of air or he might roll the bottle along the floor, stand it up and knock it down; he may do all of this whilst he is on the way to school. There are many more activities possible when he uses water with the plastic bottle. Filling and squirting, making bubbles of air, driving a floating object along the surface, experiments involving floating, sinking, creating water turbulence, moving soap bubbles, creating a fountain of soap bubbles by blowing air into the filled bottle or making it into a boat (which involves intricate details of balance). It can be made into a doll, a puppet or used as a piece of junk construction such as a lighthouse or windmill. The base could be used as a stamp for printing with paint, which could lead on to discussion of area. Different shaped bottles would lead to the building up of more complicated patterns. When the top is cut off it can serve as a water scoop, paint holder or container in which to collect specimens when on a nature walk. Two can be made into a simple balance where accuracy is not essential. Tied to a string and filled with various materials, it becomes a pendulum and with a hole in the base becomes a sand pendulum. It might have uses in physical education or be turned into maracas for use in music and movement. A collection of these would be invaluable for mathematical experiences involving shape, quantity, weight and volume. The older children can explore the properties of a cylinder and by cutting the bottle vertically or diagonally, the properties of rectangles and parallelograms. Teachers and more especially children could find many more uses for the liquid detergent bottle and it is this exploration of usage which needs to be encouraged.

The recent trend in 'in service' training seems to be to encourage the involvement of teachers in workshop situations. Here, teachers are themselves experimenting with materials; following out their own interests, developing ideas, often being shocked by their discoveries into realizing that facts which they had previously accepted are, perhaps, open to doubt and sometimes they are made aware of great gaps in their own understanding. This is a valuable personal experience.

Teachers are often anxious about testing the children's progress. The ability and stage of development of each child is constantly in the teacher's mind so that if a teacher does feel the need to assess it should be in terms of the child's own progress. Natural regression and the delicate balance of the child's health, his happiness and his

A teacher helping two children with some work on mirrors in transformation geometry.

Cooperation between two junior girls solving a maths problem.

peace of mind must be taken into account and any criticism should always be helpful and encouraging. It will often be possible to get the child to make his own criticism and if this can be done it will help him to develop pride in his work.

The teacher may find that a particular activity is not used and she will try to find the reason, perhaps withdraw some of the apparatus or provide some more attractive materials. The day to day requirements of individual children are noticed and provision made for them. To be able to provide for every member of the class, the teacher must know and understand her children well and be alert and active in the classroom.

If the whole school is working the integrated day, it is necessary for a teacher to be aware of the provisions and activities which exist in other rooms, so that she can inform a child where to go for the experience and situation he may need. When there is interchange of ideas, discussions and interplay between the groups, it helps to prevent a sense of isolation. It is the teacher's attitude to her children and her interest in them as people which gains their respect and confidence. Each classroom will reflect the teacher's character and personality and the interaction of this within the group. One important facet of the teacher's role is her diagnosis of the children's difficulties and the giving of appropriate help. These difficulties may occur on any front: social, emotional or intellectual. It is important that the teacher observes any wrong interpretations which the children make. She must discover and help with any difficulties in learning a new skill or in the development of concepts or any problems on a social or emotional level. The teacher must be continually aware of these things in the informal situation.

There is need for a constant assessment of children's responses to determine their development and their needs. Some form of written record is essential and should include all aspects of the child's development. Actual anecdotes often give more information than mere statements. It will help considerably if a record of the child is kept with relevant dated information which may concern his physical, emotional and cognitive development. If this is kept from the beginning of his school life, it will read as a biography, be of great help to each teacher who has the child in her class for the first time and be of value for reference when difficulties arise. Sources of information about a child include his parents and friends, the child's conversation, his writing and picture making, but the most valuable source is through careful observation.

If life at home, at school and at play is happy, it will reflect in the child's attitude to learning. If this attitude is strained in any way, the teacher will be aware of it. She will want to know why and will make it her urgent business to discover the reason. There are many well-tried ways of making contact with parents. PTAs, parents' evenings and arranged interviews are all very successful but any other opportunity of establishing parents' confidence in the school and gaining their cooperation should be taken. By taking a child home when he is unwell or perhaps after having an accident, by talking to a parent at the school gate or when you meet in the locality, by replying to notes sent by parents and in many other small ways avenues can be opened for easy and friendly communication between home and school. It is vital that there should be a satisfactory contact with parents. It is part of the teacher's work to have personal interviews with parents and always to be concerned that the most important adults in a child's life (his parents and his teachers) cooperate as far as possible.

Any opportunity to explain to parents the importance of refraining from criticism of the school in front of the child, should be taken. Anxiety is caused when a child's loyalty is divided. For the well being of the child, the teacher may have to resist pressure from overanxious parents and to do this she must be convinced in her own mind that what she is doing is of great value educationally. This is where the unconvinced teacher is at sea. Through reading, the teacher can learn of the psychology and philosophy which lies behind her practical work and gain confidence in her own opinions.

The teacher shares the ultimate responsibility with the parents for the growth and development of the child emotionally, physically, intellectually and aesthetically. The teacher provides a rich and interesting school environment and creates an atmosphere which will encourage thought, ideas and sincere effort on the part of the child in his activities. She is the one person to whom every child in her class can refer to as a counsellor, guide and friend and rely on for mutual understanding and respect. The children should be able to communicate ideas in every media and feel secure if they wish to reveal their innermost thoughts and feelings. She must be respected by all her children because of her interest and concern for them and they will then feel free to use their own initiative in the learning situation. A final thought to keep in mind is that we are not educating children only for their future. Education is in and for the present. Each day is an alive and exciting day in its own right, not just a preparation for some future called adulthood and earning a living and so each child's day needs to be made a whole and the whole of that day used. This is the teacher's responsibility.

CHAPTER FOUR

The child

One day, when the children were on their way out of school at the end of the afternoon, a visitor said that this scene made him even more keenly aware of the children as individuals than usual. Each afternoon the children go off down the drive singly, in twos, threes or groups, skipping now and then as they walk, some talking and laughing or perhaps looking very serious, and then scatter to their various individual homes. Next morning the children return to school, bringing the effect of their different home experiences with them and so each is a little more 'different' than they were on the previous afternoon. What do we want to do for these children whilst they are in the primary school? In 1931 the Hadow Report stated: 'What a wise and good parent will desire for his own child, a nation must desire for all children.' Teachers stand *in loco parentis* but teachers have had professional training which is not available to the wise and good parent and so their assessment of the children's needs should be more knowledgeable and obviously more objective. The children need the opportunity to be happy, to learn to live with others and not be too mistrustful of them, to be adaptable and able to cope with new situations. We want them to feel at ease and secure, to learn how to concentrate and how to work through difficulties. Children need to be accepted for themselves and not feel that they are compared or contrasted with their fellows. As teachers we want each individual child to be able to develop his fullest capacity for learning so that he will carry into adult life confidence in his ability to learn. The school must provide for each child's physical, mental, social and aesthetic development in accordance with his 'age, aptitude and ability', but in a lecture given by Ron Ablewhite of Leicester College of Education he suggested that the three Rs should be interpreted with 'the three As of Affection, Acceptance and Approval.'

In our school population we have the eager bright child, the pathetic child, the placid child, the vigorous child, the conforming child, the disturbed child, the child with a physical disability, the child who has great academic ability, the extremely sensitive child, the slow learner, the extrovert, the introvert, the culturally disadvantaged child, the child with a well developed sense of humour, the child with a flair for creativity or for science or for maths. All the labels, psychological, physical, social and intellectual and all the permutations of all the labels, can never fit any one child precisely. Each child exists as a personality different from all others and he cannot really be labelled. The individual characteristics of a child begin to emerge early in his life. His temperament responds to the mode of upbringing and he reacts to his parents and siblings and to environmental conditions in his own unique way. In considering children in any one family, reared as one would think in a similar pattern, very different personalities emerge and when the child thrusts out into a new environment of school, this will again influence his response to the world. It is so easy for a teacher to fall into the trap of labelling a child. 'Good' is a term often used by teachers to describe the conforming child who is conscientious and well behaved (although underneath this veneer he may be excessively aggressive and disliked by the other children). This label 'good' in itself is doing a disservice to the child, as so much will always be expected of him by his teachers throughout his school career. If the children are valued for themselves, they will not be judged or labelled and if they are not influenced by the fear of failing they will be more eager to experiment with new things. Each child must learn that there are certain things that he can do well but certain things which others can do better and in this way will learn to recognize and to be generous about other children's achievements.

Our children come from all types of home backgrounds and they have differing intelligence, health, temperament and tempo. Those from an unstimulating home have difficulty in progressing if provision is not made for them to have experiences of imitation and symbolic play, the feel of books, opportunities for concrete activities, spontaneous use of language, and they need to be in constant contact with a sympathetic adult. Children from more stimulating homes have perhaps already had experience of these things when they first enter school. This is one reason why there is the need for a flexible and individual approach in early school life, such as is employed in the integrated day. The child can progress at his own pace, the readiness factor is appreciated and ample use is made of the sensitive phases in his own development. Piaget stresses that there is need for 'a continuing richness of experience and challenge at an appropriate level throughout the child's development.' Each child develops at his own rate and the stages of development do not coincide with a particular age in spite of any rigidly planned standards of attainment for different age groups which some teachers try to impose. The best thing that a school can provide is a wealth of the experiences necessary to help each child in his development. Different children need varying amounts of stimulation or encouragement to persevere with a difficult task and they all need varying amounts of help in different situations.

Through activity methods the child learns by doing. With increasing experiences his confidence in himself will grow and he will begin to find out his real interests and aptitudes. When the children are allowed to follow their own interests, they are eager to learn, whereas in a formal class situation the children may have acute feelings of anxiety, inadequacy and frustration about what they do not know. As the child begins to realize his own capabilities and the things he likes best in life, he is gradually moving towards an awareness that he is an individual and is beginning to see himself in relation to others. He becomes more independent and self reliant and there is an increase in his ability to express his own ideas through activity. Children do not seem to follow a steady tempo in learning. Sometimes they need to be involved for long periods of concentrated effort to solve a particular problem. At other times they will understand something in a spontaneous flash of insight. The child of apparently very average ability often has a sudden inspiration or an illuminating flash of genius which comes as a surprise.

For the personality to develop, children must have time to be by themselves and each child needs time to be on his own, to retire within himself, to reflect and sort out his thoughts and feelings and try to make sense of the world around him. This is not usually available in a heavily timetabled or directed day. The first time he comes to the realization of his own individuality and begins to be aware of the 'I' within himself, which happens at perhaps ten or eleven years of age, we hope that he will see a self with qualities he approves and values as well as a self different from all others. The child, who has been allowed to develop his own personal traits and approach to life, who also recognizes that he must be a responsible and contributory member of society, is well on the way to becoming an adjusted, interested, educated person. As an adult this child will be able to see the shortcomings of society and possess the integrity to withstand any pressures of mass persuasion. This is one of the opportunities we hope to give him through the freedom of the integrated day for 'the best preparation for being a happy and useful man or woman is to live fully as a child.' (The Plowden Report: *Children and their Primary Schools.*)

In the past, education had the effect of subduing personalities and the discipline tended to smooth out the different characteristics of people to produce a conformity and obedience that were thought so necessary. If we stop for a moment to consider what sort of citizen is required in the twentieth century world, it is perhaps valid to say that we need a citizen who is able to adjust to new situations. He may have a colourful and lively character whilst also possessing integrity, a consciousness of the group and its needs, and a strong feeling of responsibility to society. In the integrated day situation, the child has the chance to see himself through and in his interaction with others. As he becomes aware of his influence on other people and of their influence on him, he will begin to develop this awareness, especially if the teacher does not intervene too frequently but allows the natural balance of the group to form. Successful personal relationships which are the key to a better society are seen in embryo in a well run integrated day classroom.

In the integrated day classroom the child is choosing his own tasks, developing at his own rate and working to his own best standards, so such things as copying or cheating have no point. These are ruses which children develop because they are afraid of failing to reach the imposed standard for the group. The motivation of answers marked 'right' or 'wrong' with ticks or crosses also becomes unnecessary and is quite artificial. Usually when this method of marking is employed the children spend their time chasing right answers, rather than using their intelligence to work through a problem and enjoy the intellectual activity involved.

The child needs to form a successful, loving relationship with his teacher similar to the love he has for his parents, but it is not until he begins to want to be the kind of person that the teacher would like him to be that he starts to develop his own standards of behaviour.

These standards which are in the first place the standards of the group and those of the adult of the group, become part of him. He learns self discipline. He knows that he will be justly treated and that what he thinks and feels is important and so he will learn to care for others in return. Given the opportunity to play out their anxieties, fears, insecurity and past frustrating experiences, the children will grow in emotional stability.

Each stage in education is not just a process which prepares for the next stage. The child lives in the present and each child's present needs to be a satisfactory experience. Life in a school working a successful integrated programme will be exciting and satisfying for each and every child in the group.

Whilst observing children in an integrated day situation, it is noticeable that each child has his own individual pattern and rhythm of working. Some children start work immediately they arrive in the classroom, having perhaps decided previously what they intend to do and they will have prepared for it by reading, thinking, making notes or bringing in materials. Another child may come into school with a completely open mind with no particular interest to follow. His attention will be attracted by an activity in the room and he may spend the rest of the day absorbed in his work. Another may hop from one activity to another, never becoming deeply involved in any situation. Some may decide what to do but may be unable to start without discussing their plans with a classmate or the teacher. There will be others who will be drawn into a group activity and make a useful contribution to the subject in hand. Some children will get their interest from a group and then withdraw to follow the interest alone. Occasionally a less interested child may find difficulty in involving himself in any situation. To pressurize the apparently disinterested child will only build up a resistance within him which may prove difficult to break down. The teacher should try to discover what really does interest him and whether this uninterested attitude may be symptomatic of a deeper disturbance. We hope that the children will not be afraid to have a go at most things and it is quite remarkable to notice how success in applying one idea in one situation gives added confidence to a child and he will transfer his success to another area of learning.

As the child explores the real world he relates it to his own inner mental world. He uses his inner mental images to explore reality and he is continually building each in terms of the other. As the young child brings his imagination and his fantasy life to bear in all his activity, the creative, expressive and imaginative activities cannot really be separated from learning things such as mathematics and reading.

The aggressive child needs understanding but also opportunities which allow for the release of his aggressions. Woodwork, physical activity, music and spontaneous drama allow these children to work out aggressive roles.

All the children, but especially those from homes where there is little conversation, need to have the opportunity for spontaneous and natural conversation with lots of discussion and in this way their vocabulary and understanding will grow. Through discussion, the child's ability to think and his alertness will increase.

Children who find it hard to concentrate will be able to experiment freely with various materials until they find something with which they can become really involved. They will then concentrate for longer and longer periods.

The clumsy child is the one who needs to be given jobs to do, no matter how badly he does them, because it is only in this way that he will learn to concentrate and to control his limbs.

The very capable, enthusiastic child needs a constant challenge. In some cases, this type of child's social awareness is underdeveloped or he may be emotionally unstable. In a free situation he will have a better chance to gain confidence and to learn to adjust in these spheres.

One other factor to be taken into consideration is the difference in the rate of development of boys and girls in the primary school. Practising teachers have always been aware that more boys than girls have problems involving reading, written work, concentration, self-consciousness, personal relationships and behaviour. Parents are often anxious and puzzled by this. In our experience the girls seem better able to fit into a school environment, possibly because they have adopted the female role of wanting to please. The effect of over-dependence on the mother also seems to have a less detrimental effect on a girl's ability to develop independence than in the case of a boy. Boys seem to suffer more from adverse conditions than girls. This may be because of innate differences or the expectations of the different roles that they must play in life. They each develop at different rates and react to things in different ways. It is essential that consideration of these points is given in the school situation and teachers would do well to ask themselves 'How can I gear the school environment so that boys can achieve results?' May the answer not lie in valuing the process rather than the product?

John Holt's aim for education, described in his book *How Children Fail*, is to turn children into adults who like learning so much that they will be able to learn whatever is needed. The only way he can see to do this is

> to have schools and classrooms in which each child in his own way can satisfy his curiosity, develop his abilities and talents, pursue his interests, and from the adults and older children around him get a glimpse of the great variety and richness of life. In short, the school should be a great *smörgåsbord* of intellectual, artistic, creative and athletic activities, from which each child could take whatever he wanted, and as much as he wanted, or as little.

We would add here that what the child wants and how much he wants is largely determined by his environment, and that the school and the teacher must play a vital role in this choice.

CHAPTER FIVE

The new adventure— the infant school

Before the five-year-old child actually starts full time attendance at school, he will have visited the school several times with his mother as well as spending one or more sessions there on his own. The child will have met the staff, seen much that interests him and had a brief encounter with some of the children already in the school. The headteacher has talked with the parents about the school and has discussed any anticipated difficulties. Above all, the parents have been encouraged to talk optimistically and enthusiastically with their child about the new adventure of school. These things all help children to adjust to this difficult transition from home to school.

The five-year-old child has developed both physically and mentally at an astounding rate during his pre-school years. His natural desire to master the things around him by exercising his curiosity can so easily be stifled by a school environment which makes no provision for the continuation of this self-motivated urge to explore and organize his own world. However much we try to make school a continuation of home, it is still a contrived situation but we try to plan it so that the child's whole development may continue as naturally as possible. Primarily, school must be a place where the child feels safe and secure and if he joins a vertically grouped class, perhaps one where he already has a friend, he may feel at ease more quickly. This type of group is more akin to his own experience of groups than a horizontally grouped class would be. The child enters this class at five and leaves when he is seven years of age to move to the junior school. It does in fact become his 'new family' and is for him a stable and secure social unit. Although the teacher may become a parent substitute, the child still retains the stability of the group even if a staff change does occur. If there is a personality clash perhaps between the teacher and a particular child or between two children, to move the child to another group may be advisable although in practice this is rarely necessary.

Time taken over the admission of new entrants is proved well worth while when we see how quickly they settle into the group, although even without any outward signs of distress from the child, the transition is a difficult one for him to cope with emotionally. Until he came to school, the child was in a small mixed society in familiar surroundings. Now he is joining a large group which includes a few strange adults but consists mainly of children, where the unfamiliar building, furniture, equipment, children and adults feel overwhelming.

At the other end of the age scale are the seven-year-old children who are transferred gradually to the junior school. Throughout the whole of the time in the infant school they have been frequent visitors to the junior school and are familiar with the teachers and the school layout. The teachers in the two schools talk freely together, describing with frankness the children, any problems and various aspects of education. In these ways an attempt is made to integrate the stages in the child's early education. The pre-school years merge into the infant school and the infant school years merge into the junior school.

The time spent in the infant school must be a satisfying experience for each child. This is where the process of school education begins and it is a vital part of the whole picture, important for itself and the basis of all future learning.

In the vertically grouped class the child is working with others of his own age, with younger and older children, with children of differing abilities, interests, social and economic backgrounds. He is one member of a mixed society, which by the time he joins it has become a very natural 'family' group. The pattern of the group is already formed; its culture is already in existence. This pattern is constantly undergoing almost imperceptible changes but it has a security and a tradition. In this group there is time and opportunity for a deep understanding to develop between its members including the teacher and each child. The children do not spend much of their time testing the bounds of what is allowed and what is not – finding out how far they can go – because they are soon made aware of the limits, not just by the teacher but by the established members of the class.

When we ask 'Why do children go to school?' the usual answer is 'To learn'. How do young children learn? One of the many factors involved in learning is the depth of the child's interest in the situation. Peel, in *The Psychology of Education,* writes 'The difference between real education and mere training may ultimately depend on the extent to which the child is ego-involved.' It is this personal involvement of children which is seen in a good infant school, most noticeably involvement in the expressive activities. In such a school when children are playing they are fully absorbed. Their enjoyment is obvious and yet they are making real effort. They are putting a lot of concentration into their play which has in fact similar characteristics to the work of adults. The children are working hard. They are learning through experience and are so involved and absorbed in what they are doing that this is real learning. The children will work individually at first and later form spontaneous groups, usually with friends. As the children grow older, these groups tend to form for a work purpose and will become interest groups rather than merely friendship groups. Each child has the chance to develop to the optimum of his potential and the provisions of the environment are increased in accordance with his needs. Sometimes it is necessary to modify these provisions but this should be to fit in with the need and not through any lack of equipment or materials.

The children know that they can use the materials in any way they wish. Apparatus is not strictly limited to one type of use, although one rule is that no bought apparatus or things that are expensive shall be used in any way that would damage them and that any exploitation of materials should comply with the safety rules of the classroom. For example, the children would not hesitate to use a magnet to hang from the ceiling as a pendulum but they would have to take care that no one was likely to get hurt by the swing and that the magnet would not bang against things. Children between five and seven years of age want to involve the teacher in their work very frequently and often enjoy things more if she joins in with them. They are happier about coping with strange new experiences, frustration and problems when they know that the teacher is not far away. It might be said that the teacher working with this age group carries more responsibility than with older children, since young children turn to a trusted adult more frequently. Because of this, she must always look for the subtle, gentle ways of handling any situation. For example, a boy working at the woodwork bench might start to hammer with the saw. If the teacher becomes interested in what he is making, it will be a far more effective cure than merely to prohibit and censure. When this kind of teacher is around all will be well.

There is no scheme of work as such but in a school full of materials and ideas, where the people in the environment are always alive to the many and varied possibilities in any situation, a general philosophy tends to develop. It is useful if the general points of this philosophy are recorded in written form so that the priorities may be determined and be reconsidered in the light of new experience. The teacher will also feel more security if she is clearly aware of the sequence of the stages of child development. She can use these as a foundation on which to base the trend of work and to assess the requirements of each child. The apportionment of time throughout the day is at the teacher's discretion as is judgement of the needs of the group. She feels free to call the children together whenever necessary. These collective times involving either a small group or sometimes the whole class are used for such things as discussion, help with a technical point, preparation, story, poetry appreciation, religious education, physical education, movement or music. Each teacher usually finishes with a short time such as this to give a quiet relaxed ending to the school day. There is a tidying up of the room before noon and a general clear up before the end of the day. The children do not have the traditional playtime although the teachers do have a break for coffee. The school assembly is at 11.15 each morning and is usually taken by the children themselves and involves some interest which has arisen in their classroom.

On one particular Monday morning, the outside doors of the school are opened as soon as several teachers have arrived and the children stream in. David has brought some metal shavings in fanciful and modernistic shapes. Rosemary has a bunch of wild flowers. Susan brings a bag of bacon rinds for the bird food shop and Peter a bag filled with milk tops. 'I am going to make a rattly caterpillar out of these,' he says as he walks past. 'I saw it on the television on Friday night.'

The children go to their rooms and start to work. Last Friday in Room 1 Michael, Alan and Gary finished making a scooter and a car at the woodwork bench. Today they have launched straight into plans for setting up a motor show. They have brought toy cars from home and are planning show stands, price labels and catalogues. June and Yvonne are soon playing the guessing game which they invented a few days ago. First, Jane takes a handful of acorns and shows them briefly to Yvonne. Yvonne guesses how many there are and then Jane counts them in secret. If Yvonne has guessed accurately she has the acorns. If not, Jane will say 'Less' or 'More' and Yvonne guesses again. This game has held their attention for half an hour each day since they first invented it. Bridget has put on an apron, rolled up her sleeves and started to work at the clay table. Michael C and Raymond are working with the building blocks again this morning. For some days they have been involved with constructing bridges of all types and materials. Today, from Room 2, the teacher has brought in the wooden construction arch which stands on its own when a supporting board is removed. The principle of the keystone seems quite new to the boys and they are intrigued. Over at the six foot zinc bath containing water, Carol, Jill, Margaret and Cynthia have a mountain of bubbles and are chatting with excitement about the colours and reflections in them. 'My Mummy had a bubble bath at the week end. She'd had it in her drawer since last Christmas. Mummy said it made her feel real rich and scrumptious. After, she let me go in but there were only little bubbles then.' The four girls, talking, role playing, observing and learning, continue with the session of playing with the toy dolls and the bubbles.

Paul came straight in and read the thermometer, recorded a temperature of 60 degrees on the chart and now he goes to put the thermometer in the sun for another reading. This is a regular first job for Paul each day. He then goes to join Rodney. They take the box of mechanical junk out on to the veranda to construct various intricate buildings and works. Now they have wires attached to the woodwork table 'to blow it up'. Theresa is working in the painting corner. She is a five-year-old with bright auburn hair and at present painting is her first love. She always produces two paintings each time that she goes to paint. She leaves one for school and carefully dries and folds the other 'for Mummy'. A group of children are over by the window chatting. In the music corner, Helen is struggling to work out the tune 'Summer Good bye' on the chime bars. She learns to play a new tune each week as do a further six children in the class. They also compose their own tunes and words and write out the music using the letter names of the notes. Helen is beginning to learn to read musical notation too. Cynthia and Louise are continuing the frieze to illustrate the story of the 'Twelve Princesses who Danced their Shoes to Pieces' and Ann is writing a précis of the story to attach to the picture. Peter is starting work on his rattly caterpillar. Elizabeth is writing and drawing something which looks like a comic strip. This is her favourite way of presenting her ideas.

The teacher is busy with the dinner book and register chores but still has an eye for what the children are doing. 'Cynthia, just tie Theresa's apron, please.' Peter seems to be getting frustrated with trying to thread the milk tops on to string and needs some help to get on with his rattly caterpillar and this is where the teacher goes first. She then steps in as she hears Alan, Gary and Michael A discussing the possibility of bringing their pedal cars from home for the motor show. There is not much space in the classroom and the boys agree to bring them on a fine day so that the show can be set up outside.

Bridget brings her clay model to the teacher with a piece of white card. 'It's a giffy. Please write It's a giffy' is all she says and then she takes the model which looks like a 3D model of the inner ear to put on a shelf for the other children to see. The teacher is now with the children using water and joins in the conversation about bubbles. And so the day has started.

A little later in the morning an exhibition is in full swing with children from other rooms coming to look round. They pay a shilling for a 'catalogue'. Jane and Yvonne went on to do various computations with the acorns they had been using for their guessing game and then Jane decided to plant one of them in the garden. Whilst she was digging she found an easel clip in the soil. The metal had rusted through exposure and a group of children talked with each other and with the teacher about this. David has built a triangular tower with the metal shavings and the magnets and is now sketching the shapes. Yvonne has moved into the library corner. She has read a story aloud to the teacher and they have discussed the content. Now Yvonne has chosen an easier book. She gathers Theresa who is also in the book corner and begins to read a story to her. Soon, a group of younger children are sitting round Yvonne listening to her story and later this turns into a game of school. The games of school are played in the traditional way with an authoritarian teacher and naughty children. Jane now asks if she and Peter, who has finished his caterpillar, can dig over another part of the garden and plant the anemone corms which were brought to school last week. Gordon helps them to read the

Two infant girls exploring the world of capacity in the water corner.

Group discussion of a tricky point during a cookery assignment in the infant school.

Juniors doing various woodwork jobs in the open air. When the weather allows as much work as is possible takes place out of doors.

A group of juniors experimenting with electricity.

label on the packet. 'Plant 1½ inches deep, two together, points downwards.' Half an hour later the two boys and the girls come in with the problem, 'We've got five left. How do we do it in twos now? We shall have one left over,' and the teacher works with these children discussing odd and even numbers.

Rodney and Paul have now involved two more boys in making a mechanical man. Then they spend some time doing a play about robots and later come rushing in asking: 'Can we make two big ones out of boxes?' They search the school for suitable big boxes, egg crates and wire and by late afternoon, two life sized robots called Percy and Jimmy are brought into the cloakroom out of the rain and the group are dictating stories involving Percy and Jimmy in all kinds of adventures. As they go home that evening, Rodney says: 'Stay there Jimmy until tomorrow and don't get up to trouble in the night' and to the teacher: 'Hope you have time to type our stories tonight because I think I shall be able to read them all.'

To describe all the work that has gone on in the room during that one day would be an impossibility. There has been so much. The children are tired but have gained tremendous satisfaction from their day.

The teacher is temporarily exhausted but is already going over some of the happenings, making notes and thinking ahead to the provision she must make for tomorrow.

It would be a good idea to bring the prisms in again tomorrow from the science corner in the hall.
Those girls at the bubbles this morning were getting interested in the spectrum.

And the teacher makes notes on her pad.

1 Prisms
2 Pictures and books about robots
3 Type stories
4 Cooking day tomorrow. Cooking materials?
5 Robot music, perhaps electronic

The teacher then tries to recapture the significant points of the day.

When Yvonne was working from the book *How to Make a Doll's Dress* she was confusing twice as big with half as big. I must remember that tomorrow and see how I can help her towards understanding this point.

When Jane, Elaine and Peter read today they were all having trouble with two-syllable words although they were making some good guesses in context. I will find five or ten minutes for this tomorrow and work with all three.

What else have I to remember?

Felt and beads to add to the clay table. Bridget seems to be developing a modernistic bent here and it will perhaps give her some new ideas.

A further supply of bulbs and batteries so that the boys can light up the mechanical men. They were frustrated today when the batteries would not work.

Now for the children's individual records. What points need to be written down?

Ian's record. Ian was using the balance and various materials for weighing. He had the balance equally weighted and he said 'Look they are the same levelment.' This seemed an interesting word to use and we spent some time discussing just what he did mean. He then went on to do a dozen other 'levelments' and recorded pictorially what he had done.

Paul's record. Paul was working with peg boards, pegs and scales and mapping various results that he worked out. He came to fetch me to see what he had just discovered and explained it by saying: 'I am silly, I went to all the trouble of weighing a hundred pegs and they weighed four ounces and then I weighed fifty pegs and they weighed two ounces. I needn't have weighed those fifty because fifty is half of a hundred so it's just got to be two ounces or it's nearly two ounces.'

Five-year-old David's record. David has been indulging in particularly aggressive play in the house corner. Helen seems to have some influence with David. I heard her discussing with him in a very calm and helpful way and reasoning with him about this aggressive behaviour.

Geoffrey. I had a short but very interesting conversation with Geoffrey's father this morning. Geoffrey's account of Daddy buying a grocer's shop which has dominated his conversation for the past week is complete fantasy. He had everything so logically worked out that we were all completely convinced that it was real. Geoffrey is perhaps lonely. He is an only child with older parents than is usual, an exceptionally gifted boy but doesn't seem to have many friends. Perhaps he needs to be with someone who has a similar exceptional ability. Will check the possibilities.

And so the teacher continues. She writes in the children's records anything she feels is significant. When the notes are finished she plays the tape recorder through and as well as the stories hears a long verbal account of Susie's day out. Susie is only just six and her account shows an amazing grasp of time, space and causal relationships.

The next day in they come and again the school is soon a hive of industry. In Room 2, an interest in the fun fair has developed. It started when Billy made six aeroplanes out of wood and with the help of some old pram wheels turned them into an aeroplane ride. This gave some of the boys an idea. They wrote a list of things which they wanted in a funfair and they set about making them. The list was largely influenced by what they had available or knew they could make or obtain. Now they have a hoopla stall, a ghost house, famous cricketers, Funny Mirrors, The Aeroplane Ride, Roll on Pink, a helter skelter and a toffee-apple stall. A bank was set up and Spencer, the bank manager, organized a sytem of giving out the money to the customers and recording in a bank book. He made the stallholders bank each shilling they took as they took it. It was laborious but the children made it work. Tickets which were available at each stall helped the children to record their experiences and spending. Almost every class has now produced a funfair book. This was one interest which involved reading, writing, maths, conversation, science, art, music and drama in one integrated situation.

In Room 3, a group of children are arranging a party. The food includes sandwiches of mustard and cress which they have grown on flannel and lettuce in their own garden. They are having jelly, jam tarts and peppermint creams. Some children in the school cook each day and sell the produce afterwards but today the children are busy cooking for their party. Mary, who is in charge of the greengrocery shop, has discovered that the potatoes are sprouting and has put some on the nature table to grow in a saucer of water. Here Stephen is carefully explaining to Richard that 'if you take one of these dandelion seeds and plant it you will get dandelions.' The gerbils in Room 3 have produced six babies and David is drawing the family of baby gerbils. A group of children are intrigued by tricks and puzzles and there have been a mass of constructions with bricks which have places containing hidden treasure. There have been many pictures with a puzzle element and headed 'What's wrong?' A list of answers has been compiled on a separate page. This has led the children on to making maps of islands with written clues to finding hidden treasure. Hazel brought her tortoise to school and the children became interested in reptiles, snakes and lizards. Simon and Stephen are busy writing their space stories. 'If things on the moon are one sixth of their weight on earth, I'll make this rocket 6 tons so that it will only weigh 1 ton on the moon. That's easiest,' he reasons. I find myself trying to check if his first assumption is correct or not but it doesn't matter to Simon whether it is fact or fantasy. A boy working at the mirror table has made a corridor of reflections and Daphne is alternating between flashing reflections of sunlight round the room and horrifying her friends with their change of appearance as seen in the metal glazing sheet which she bends into a convex or concave shape. John is chatting on the telephone to Gary in Room 4. In this room the children are off to visit a farm and are patiently waiting for the bus to arrive. Some parents are going along too.

In Room 5, there are some children painting and decorating the Wendy House and some busy sewing. They are making glove puppets and cushions and one little girl is making a cat out of fur fabric. Another group of children is working on a collage of Albert the Dragon and a collage of the sun is being made from coloured magazine paper. As we move round the school we see milk bars in every room where the children can drink their milk at any time during the morning. There are shops of all kinds, a castle, a hospital, a clinic, an Indian encampment and a dark house. The dark house is a great favourite and numbers using it need to be strictly limited. This is equipped with torches, bulbs and batteries, small toys, card, etc. Tape recordings taken of the conversation in the dark house are fascinating and some really worthwhile discussion happens in here. The children tried to make shadows and shadow puppets in the dark house, but the source of light was not strong enough and eventually the projector lamp was pressed into service. In one room, there is a bus station with a café where the menu reads: 'Eggs, bacon and sausage. Chips, roast beef, potatoes, peas, brussels. Steamed chocolate pudding and custard.' The children who visited the Jewry Wall Museum last week are making mosaics. One is made of rice, peas and butter beans. Timothy and Mark have drawn a life size skeleton and the influence of the museum visit is seen in many of the activities in the room. David is at the sand tray as we walk past. The children have a funnel full of sand and they watch as the dry sand falls through the funnel. 'Look,' says David, 'it makes a slow hole in the sand.' The sand gathers from the edges of the funnel and forms a slight vortex before trickling out through the hole. 'It's not like water is it?' 'No, that makes a quick hole.' Then he pauses for a moment as he watches. 'And it doesn't pile up afterwards, either.'

On the veranda of Room 6, at the water trolley which is made of transparent plastic, the children are playing with bottles. They are using them as imaginary divers and making bubbles as they go under the water. The children are constructing an authentic-looking wreck at the bottom of the trolley. 'You can't use that wood to make the wreck, it's not soggy enough to sink.' The wreck is eventually constructed mainly from metal. 'Why didn't you make a boat first and then sink it?' the teacher asked. 'Because it's sunk already and the divers have just found it.' Later that day however there was a lot of interesting work involving sinking and floating and a fleet of boats were constructed designed to sink quickly, or slowly, or not at all. Susan is stroking Winnie the guinea pig as she sits with her on her lap. Raymond and John are working with a board balanced on a fulcrum. They are building with poleidoblocs on either end or in the middle and devising various balance problems between them. In Room 7 last week, large areas of the floor where water had been spilled were covered with newspaper and as the teacher put the sheets down she said 'I wonder how many sheets I am going to need', and this one question started some children on an inquiry into area. How many sheets to cover the whole room? How many half sheets? How many triangular pieces of newspaper? They went on to make a plan of the school, using squares of sticky paper. Today these same boys are trying to sort out how the water system in the school works. They are following the piping from place to place and mapping it out on a large sheet of paper. The twins are working with a sand pendulum and Tina is writing. She is stopping now and then to frown and bite the end of her pencil. On inquiring 'What's the trouble, Tina?' the teacher is told: 'I'm just trying to remember the things I did last Sunday morning before I had my dinner. I'm trying to put them down in the right order and I'm a bit mixed up.' Room 6 has one table full of all kinds of springs. Pictures and paintings of spirals adorn the walls. Marjorie is playing with the slinky on the steps. 'He really walks down steps you know,' she tells me. The children using the sand tray have used plastic to form a container for water to make a lake and a stream. 'What is your stream doing?' asks the teacher. 'It's twisting and turning and trickling round corners,' says David slowly as he traces the course of the water with his finger. 'Yes, it's meandering along very gently,' says the teacher. Mary and Angela have a bowl of water into which they are dropping spots of food colouring with a pipette as they swirl the water round and round with a stick. 'Ooh, a whirlpool, look, and look now.' Some of the paintings and work show that the children have recently visited the local church. Semi-transparent chocolate cases have been used to transform two windows into stained glass and Joan has made a drawing of the way to church. The label underneath reads: 'It is a puddly way, a lumpy way, a long way to the church.' Jill and Sally are 'making a film' about the visit on a roll of paper.

The teacher in Room 9 has gone for her coffee but as we move into the room and look around Graham is numbering the houses on the map of the street where he lives and Doreen is setting the table in the Wendy House 'for Mummy, Daddy, Granny and the little girl'. Heather and a group of smaller children are playing at weddings. This is a game which seems to have spanned the centuries. Some other children are completing block graphs which record the number of pets kept by children in school. Several are fascinated as they watch the worm tracks from sand to soil in the glass fronted wormery and Keith is sitting under the teacher's table 'just thinking'. Raymond has collected some of the biggest snails he could find and is watching the trails they make across a piece of glass. When he has finished he will carefully return them to where he found them. The children have a self discipline and a commitment to the task in hand which is independent of the presence of the teacher and so carry on for this short period of her absence as if nothing had changed. In a formal situation the teacher's absence would have the opposite effect and she would be the chief influence controlling the learning and the behaviour by personal authority which her absence would remove.

It is a bright day and some of the children are outside playing with shadows. They are playing various forms of the game 'Chase the Shadow', drawing round each other's shadows, marking a spot on the playground and trying to make their shadow touch this spot. Many of the children are working at woodwork benches outside or at water trays. There are children building, gardening, working out situations in spontaneous drama and searching for insects, whilst some are sitting in the sunshine with a book. Several children are busily examining the tree which has recently been felled in the front of the school to make way for a car park. The insects, the different types of wood, the leaves, the roots are a source of constant wonder and discovery. Richard and Mark are counting the vehicles which pass the school using tallies of different kinds for cars, vans and lorries. Traffic is quite light but there is a lot of conversation about transport. When the bus arrives to take the children to the farm there is great excitement. Some time later Richard and Mark translated their tallies into representations of vehicles and made a chart of the morning's activity. A group of children on one of the verandas is playing with bubble tubes using various liquids and small articles to fill them and make bubbles in the tube. They are making the liquid move slowly or quickly and setting themselves all kinds of problems to sort out and solve. There is great excitement here because this is the first day this equipment has been introduced into the class. Simon and Stephen are making records about the birds which visit the bird table, using a tape recorder and a box camera. Their observation is keen and perceptive. Everywhere there are young children working, talking, expressing, creating, learning and thinking.

Each class in the infant school could easily become a closed unit working in isolation and care is taken to see that movement between different areas is easy and free. The use of areas outside the classroom such as verandas and corridors helps, for here the children mingle freely. The children also visit each other's rooms and some stay for quite long periods in a class to which they do not strictly belong. The teachers know what is being done in other rooms and help each other with ideas or the provision of materials. The classroom doors are rarely closed. Certain large or expensive apparatus is perhaps only available in one room but is freely borrowed for use in other classes as an addition to that which the rooms possess already. It is not necessary for all types of apparatus to be available in every room and as this school is naturally divided into three parts with three rooms in each part, a system has been worked out so that certain activities may only be available in one of the three rooms. The basket of large bricks perhaps available in one of the rooms, woodwork in the second and clay in the third. This means that children must move to another room to use these materials. Not only does it cut down on the activities which any one teacher must attend to, but also aids the movement of children between rooms and means that these things can be used on a larger scale and in greater depth.

A storeroom with a concrete floor has been turned into a clay room where a small group of children can use clay freely and the staff have organized a junk area where everyone brings any waste materials which may be useful in school. This central store means that children are able to have a wide selection of junk materials for their constructions. There is a communal collection of dressing up clothes which is kept in the central part of the school and is run as a dressing up shop. Musical instruments, science equipment as well as fiction and reference books are all available in a central area. The staffroom library of books about education and reference books for the teachers is well used. A volunteer group of mothers spends an afternoon in the school helping to make and maintain books and equipment. Those who have children who are four years of age bring them along to form a playgroup in the school. On these days the older children have less space available for their use, but for the rest of the time children use the foyer which is full of books and equipment; the corridors where there is a row of shops, tables with typewriters and xylophones for the children's use, the entrance hall steps, the staffroom, the hall when it is available and even the headteacher's office. The sculpture of a donkey by Willi Soukop is a great favourite. He gives rise to much spontaneous drama but is also sought out by some of the older children as a place to sit and read. A group of children is usually to be found round the aquarium, terrapin tank and animal corner observing, sketching, making notes or just talking and there are others engrossed in exploring the material on various display tables. It is essential that most of the displays put out on tables should be of the kind that children are allowed to handle. The static beauty or colour corner, which is very carefully arranged and not to be touched, does serve a purpose but must be changed at least once a week to be really worth while. On the whole, just looking is not really enough for the young child. Taped stories are available for the children to come to listen to at any time in the day. These tape recorders have been adapted as purely playback machines with earphone attachments.

One day Howard, Andrew and Brian, three very mature boys, each from different classes in the school, started a club and set up the headquarters in a corner of the entrance hall. Over a period of time their activities have included bird spotting, collecting car numbers, writing a weekly paper, making a wild flower collection and organizing an art exhibition. They kept a diary of club events and were continually amending the rules. They then wrote a serial story which they dramatized at a later date. It was a version of King Arthur and his Knights. Howard had recently been to Tintagel in Cornwall. The children seemed to enjoy the jousting. The knights were made out of cardboard and strung up across the hall. This seemed to be the best part of the play for them. The knights were outlines of various men visitors to the school. They had cajoled delivery men and official visitors into lying down so that their outlines could be traced and the templates were then suitably accoutred with armour, helmets, etc.

Approximately two thirds of the children stay at school for lunch and this time is made as much a part of the day as possible. At lunch time the children come into the dining hall freely when they have washed and sit wherever they wish. A teacher is at the head of each table and serves the children at the table as a family group. Children also help with serving. No external pressures are put on the children; they chat quite naturally, clear dishes and serve the second course as each particular table is ready and when they have finished, the teacher will say grace with her own table and the children disperse easily and naturally. The whole mealtime has an easy and relaxed atmosphere. There is always a steady hum of conversation but rarely any excessive noise.

Subject barriers and divisions of time do not and could not exist in this school with such a dynamic atmosphere. The children's interests and needs are the determining factor, not the timetable and subjects. Questions which will inevitably be asked relating to the wasting of time, one-sided development, acquiring skills and standards are dealt with in other parts of the book but one point deserves a further mention. Some people insist that laziness is encouraged when infant children work in this free way. Mentally and physically normal children are not naturally lazy. If they are, it is symptomatic of some deeper malady which the environment may be reinforcing. Laziness is not something which stands alone. The child starts to be lazy as a reaction to something in his environment and whilst the cause is present so also will be the laziness.

In a successful integrated day, children of all ability levels are encouraged to develop their powers of initiative and resourcefulness and to enjoy work. They find learning exciting and attractive for it involves watching things grow, working with living things, examining things, taking them to pieces, watching things move and change, satisfying their curiosity, solving problems, seeing the effect they can have on materials, acquiring skills, constructing, creating and expressing. This may seem to be play, but they are also ready and willing to do a certain amount of repetition and practice when they can see the reason for this.

It is in the infant school that children first begin to learn about personal relationships. Often, an excellent relationship exists between the teacher and the child. These are conditions at their best for successful learning. Sometimes the child finds his first security through the materials or apparatus provided and it will only be later as the teacher involves herself in his activity with materials that the child will begin to develop a *rapport* with her.

The children have the opportunity for social experience with their peers and the teacher encourages this interaction. She does not step in and prohibit every time she sees children starting to argue, for they will never learn about interaction for themselves unless they experience it personally. She does however have set and consistent bounds beyond which no child can go. One of the first lessons that a child must learn in a large group is that he has to take turns with others. With understanding and help, the child soon begins to develop a responsibility for his own behaviour rather than relying on outside authority and control. It is far more difficult to be self disciplined than to rely on authority just as it is more difficult for some children to choose than to be told what to do. Teachers sometimes have to give more direction than usual to a few children during their first term in school so that they are not overwhelmed by the insecurity of having to decide for themselves what they will do.

Some children can use language fluently and expressively when they come to school but some have a very limited use of language. Although most children by the age of five can understand simple expressions used by adults, there are some who cannot make sentences and others who cannot make themselves understood. The talk, extension of vocabulary and language which goes on in infant schools today is particularly essential for these children. So much depends on language. If the child's home background has provided only limited experiences, he will need compensatory exercises. If the child's home background has provided only limited experiences, he will need compensatory experiences. The teacher may be the first interested adult willing to work with the child and answer his questions. If his preschool experience has not helped him to have a certain control over his emotions and if his relationships with the adults around him have been unsatisfactory, this too will seriously interfere with his ability to learn.

These are some of the points which are uppermost in the teacher's mind when the children first enter school. She asks herself 'What is this particular child's stage of development and what are his immediate needs?' Once in school, each child progresses at a different rate. So many things influence his rate of development and the teacher needs to be sensitive to every facet of the child's character and temperament, know the influences of his background and be able to define in words his present stage of development. The teacher with sensitivity can almost predict any one child's response to a given situation.

At this point it might be useful to take each facet of learning traditionally associated with the first two years in school and explore the possibilities of their development within the integrated framework. Whilst staff do not see total experience divided into areas of learning, they still bear in mind that if there is to be progression the teacher must focus on the general direction of development in certain areas.

Communication is the priority of the school. There is communication between the adult and the child, between the adults themselves and between the children. The child communicates with himself in and through all his expressive activities. Through this he learns more about himself and the world, but expressive activities also communicate to others whether the child would wish it or not. The facial muscles of the young child have not yet assumed control over the expressions which show his feelings and his actions usually betray his intent. In most cases the young child seems to need to involve a human partner in his ventures. He communicates his feelings and ideas both to children and adults through language and other media.

The children are free to have spontaneous and natural conversation throughout the day. This is not just limited to chatter and real discussion often develops where the children get involved and need to give and receive clear explanations. Children's questions are talked over and the teacher's questions to the child are designed to encourage him to think more deeply and express himself more clearly. From this verbal expression, the child steps into the world of written expression. Whilst he is talking excitedly about an experience, the teacher might note some of the phrases he uses and write them down. Children express ideas in drawing and the teacher often extends this by adding a phrase to the drawing. Children record talk on the tape recorder and the teacher writes or types this out. Spoken language comes to be associated with writing in many ways. Reading and writing begin to have a meaning and a purpose through writing letters, captions and notices and right from the beginning language is seen as a means of communicating feeling as well as fact. The child writes when he has something to write about and so it will be lively and exciting. He remembers the feelings associated with this first hand experience which he wants to tell others about. Reading and writing in these early stages develop together. The child reads what he has written and usually at this age writes so that it will be read, although there is no insistence on the work being read if the child feels he does not wish it. The long term aim is to have the children talk and write naturally, freely and expressively, to love and appreciate books and reading and to have confidence in their ability to cope with language. Because of this, the approach to language learning is made as anxiety-free as possible. Any difficulties are looked into and the cause diagnosed as soon as possible.

No set approach is used in the teaching of reading. Practising teachers are very aware of when a child shows interest in learning to read and the readiness factor is readily appreciated. Where one approach may be the most successful for one child, it can be less successful with another. The teacher decides which is the best individual approach for each child. Some may need the security of a graded series of readers and some may not. Once the child has started to learn to read, it is important that he feels he is making progress and succeeding. A diagnosis is made of any who appear ready to read but do not seem to progress. Children reach a point of understanding where a few weeks will see them pass from apparent non-reading to near fluency and if sufficient help is available at this sensitive period the mastery of reading will be comparatively swift and painless. This usually happens in the infant school but often in the first year of the junior school when the age division between the two schools is as early as seven years. Reading habits which are developed as children may persist throughout life and it is important that the child learns to read with comprehension. There are certain young children who prefer to read 'in their head' and too much emphasis should not be placed on making them speak aloud everything they read.

Typewriters are used by the children and many who have kinaesthetic difficulties enjoy this swift and effective adult way of recording. When the children start to write for themselves, all sorts of ways are employed for them to find the correct spelling of words but this is not allowed to interfere with the free flow of ideas and much of the spelling is wildly incorrect though often ingenious.

The stories and poetry presented to the children are always carefully chosen. Sentimental or morbid poetry or stories are strictly avoided although many are chosen which help the children to an awareness of the thoughts, needs and feelings of other people. Books are chosen for their attractiveness of language, illustration, presentation and appeal to children.

There is always opportunity for natural and spontaneous dramatic activity which takes the form of miming, dressing up, acting out roles and experiences in imaginative play and making up plays. This is a very necessary and vital part of the child's life in school.

Puppetry too, is used by the children as a form of dramatic expression. The children use shadow puppets, glove puppets and marionettes. The younger children enjoy the puppets quickly made from a circle of card with a tab for the finger and a handkerchief draped round the hand. Some of these puppets the children make themselves, but often they want to pay immediate attention to the dramatic, rather than to spend time making the puppets and so factory made puppets are always available. The children spend much of their time in the school working with creative media. In this sphere, too, we are prepared to allow the child to work at his own stage and not ask for a standard beyond his development. In constructional activities, children all go through a phase of experiment and their first models may be badly constructed and crude but the child will later pay more attention to accuracy and will spend time searching for the material which is exactly right to make the finish he has decided upon. The children are told of the origin of the raw materials they use and are encouraged to think about the materials in terms of colour and the effect of light, shape and texture. The use of the right language often helps the child to express his ideas in artistic media. The children use clay and dough to produce realistic and abstract models. They make and dress dolls and puppets, make sewing pictures and enjoy woodwork. Involved in all these activities, as well as the creative and imaginative elements, are such things as the development of muscular coordination, mathematics and design and the development of language. The children express their experiences and ideas in painting and collage work. The teacher does not impose her own ideas on their work but always shows interest and enthusiasm. Motivation through discussion and physical experience may produce more vital work but this should not be overdone.

In the school where there is no division of time into subjects, mathematical problems and problems of all kinds are part of the natural and total experience of the child. They are meaningful because they exist in the real, concrete, everyday situations of life in the school and the children are enthusiastic about learning how to solve these problems. A quotation from the Ministry of Education Handbook of Suggestions published in 1938 reads: 'Where a child has the reason to experiment in a suitable environment, number ideas occur spontaneously without formal teaching and without difficulty,' and yet in 1968 many people find this hard to believe and achieve.

In the progressive school, the child learns to solve problems as they arise rather than being led through planned stages in a vacuum. Some of these problems will be primarily concerned with mathematics. The planned stages in learning arithmetic used to start with computation. Learning tables was the next step and problems were presented which were usually quite divorced from first hand experience. This learning depended to a great extent on memory and rote learning without any real understanding. When the children come to school they will all have had very different backgrounds of mathematical experience. This is the starting point for each child and the school aims to add to his experience through his activity. Accurate terminology is always used and the child's discoveries and ideas are recorded. Recording of concrete experience is represented pictorially perhaps involving mapping or block graphs. In the total school situation the child has experience of sorting, ordering, matching and pattern play, counting and grouping. He is made aware of relationships, size and shape. Symbols are not used until the teacher knows that they will have meaning for the child and he will understand them. 'Playing with bricks' is one phrase which rouses emotion in critics of this freer way of working, but working with materials, building and construction of all kinds, enables the child to discover many relationships of quantity, equality and inequality, similarity and dissimilarity and to experiment with balance. For example, in building, the child will think about such things as having walls of similar height and length or bridges with level supports. Some building materials are also designed so that a certain number of units is equivalent to a larger unit. 'Bricks' also include poleidoblocs, logic blocks or other structured mathematical apparatus which although not used in any formal sense are played with constructively and the children's ideas extended by the teacher.

There is an element of measuring in most things. Relationships, proportional comparisons and assessments are more important than exact measurement and as in all things, measuring is more meaningful if used for a purpose (e.g. how much hose to go along a corridor to reach a sink). Time is a difficult concept for the young child and he will not fully comprehend this until he is older but the children enjoy timing with a pinger such daily happenings as the time it takes to put up the PE apparatus or to tie shoe laces or the time it will take for the cakes to be cooked.

In the infant school water, dry sand and wet sand are in constant use and part of their function is to help children towards the awareness of the conservation of quantity.

There are shops of every kind, and money is used in many play situations. The shops are planned to give worthwhile shopping situations. Whatever is sold can be used as an added piece of equipment in the room, for example, there is a dressing up clothes shop, a games shop, a toy shop, a shop selling pots and pans for use in the Wendy house, a dolls' clothes shop, etc. The teacher aims to provide many varied experiences which will lead the child towards understanding mathematical concepts. She varies, extends or limits the stimuli according to the needs of the children concerned, and talks with them about their experiences. Mathematical experiences arise in PE, movement, art and in all things as the teachers are constantly drawing the attention of the children to the mathematical possibilities of the environment.

Mathematics and science are closely linked. The children are undirected in their exploration of science materials. They are having their first experience of many things – the first time they see the spectrum in a prism, the delight at playing with magnets, the joy in taking something to pieces. Children love to experiment with air and water, sound, light, time, magnets, pulleys, ramps and levers. They are eager to know about temperature, shadows, ice, snow and sunshine. These interests arise spontaneously both in and out of school and the children are encouraged to inquire and to observe accurately. Nature is a subject which offers great scope for the children. They are fascinated by all the common natural objects around them, by animals, plants, insects and flowers. The children are given the opportunity to observe for themselves by having living things in the school, by growing things and by using the whole natural environment.

Religious education is based on living together as a community and is associated with everyday happenings which have meaning for the child in his home and school situations. A service, at 11.15 each day, is taken by the children and centres round some topic which has arisen in the classroom. To it they bring ideas, paintings, models, collections of things, their own prayers, poems and choice of hymns. Hymns are carefully chosen for the quality of the music and language and must have an easily understood content. Many of the more suitable hymn tunes have been given fresh words.

Music involves the children singing, often orchestrating their songs with percussion instruments, using instruments freely to experiment with tunes, composing airs and fitting words to their compositions, experimenting with rhythm and sound and listening to all kinds of music. Children who are interested work in groups at Carl Orff type music. An old piano has been made available for the children's use and one teacher who plays the guitar is often surrounded by children singing or listening as she plays. A group of thirty children are learning to play the recorder.

Whilst the integrated day ideally includes children using PE equipment and apparatus freely, which is available at all times, there is still a place for the group lesson in PE and dance. These lessons which the teacher takes occasionally, extend the children's ideas and this helps them when they are working alone. Children experiment

Two junior boys working together with building blocks.

Two boys sharing mathematical equipment but working on their own.

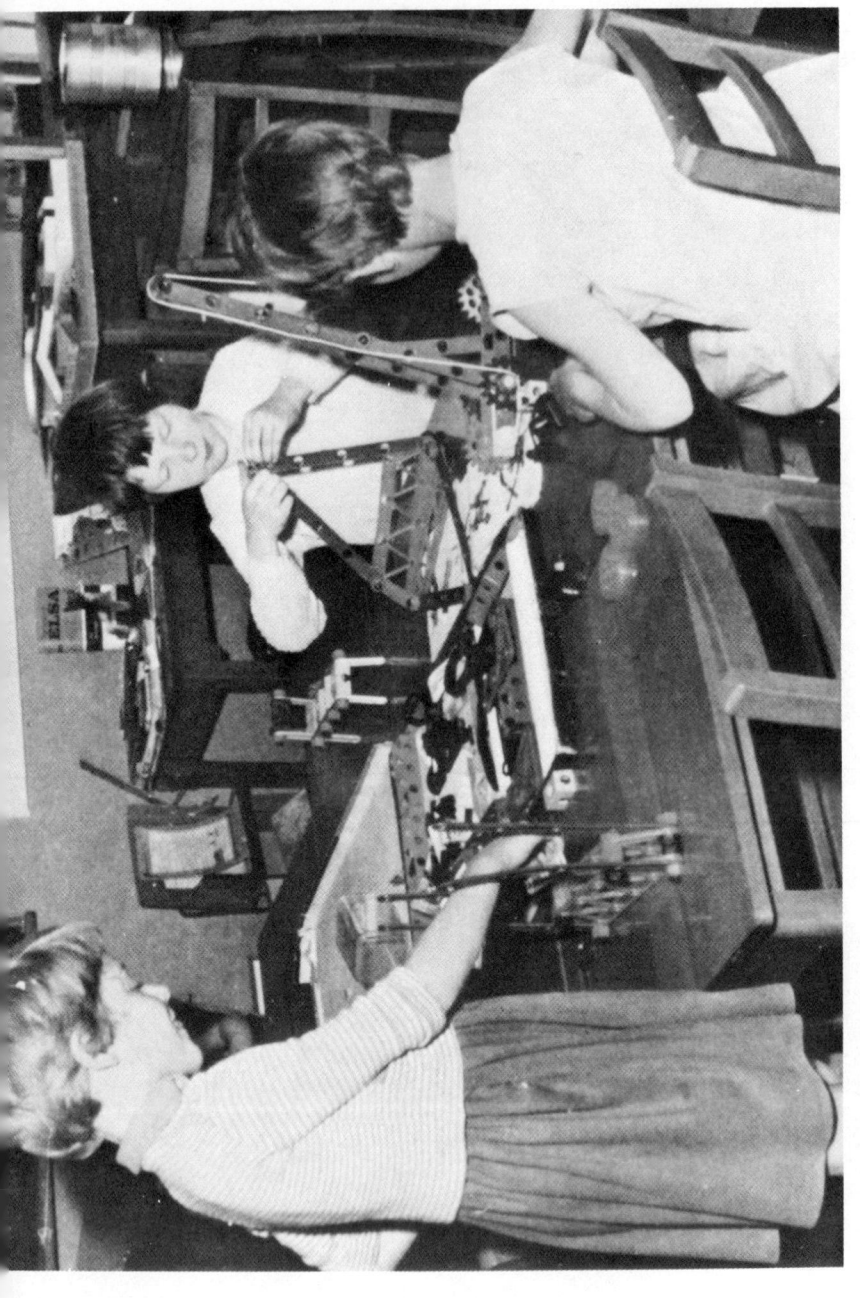

Girls enjoy making mechanical models just as much as boys.

freely with movement, with instruments and dressing-up clothes during the day. Their movement is natural and spontaneous and they also respond to suggestions and react to stimuli. Group movement lessons which are frequently taken are based on and involve the use of the body in time, weight and space. The children are never asked to be 'giants' or be a 'tree' but to feel the qualities of a tree, the strength of it, the forceful roots twisting into the ground, the slow growth and the stretched upward reaching feel of the branches. Visual imagery and vocabulary are vital aids to suggestion. Story themes, noises, sounds, records and percussion are used as stimuli to movement.

Each term, when the new children have had a certain amount of time to settle into school routine, we start in our school what we call 'All Change' sessions. For one whole session, each room provides one definite type of work. At present in Room 1 we are lucky enough to have a teacher who speaks fluent French and she runs a French room. This may be conversation, singing, running a French café, looking at pictures of French people and scenes, books and newspapers. The other rooms use such things as art, mathematics, dance, science, music making, dramatic activity and language. The room is still primarily active, concerned with exploration rather than giving information. For instance, the language room would have discussion groups, taped stories, tape recording, typing, writing and a library. The children who opt for music, as well as using various instruments in composing and orchestrating, listening and studying sounds, also have some help from a teacher from the junior school who helps them to learn to play the descant recorder. The teachers are in charge of the subject which they most enjoy but do change the bias of the room frequently. The children choose the room in which they wish to spend the session. Numbers must be controlled and the teachers give children a ticket on which the room number and the child's name is written. Children must go to the same room for at least two sessions. When the children return to their own classroom the teacher keeps the card until the next 'All Change' session. After two sessions in one room are recorded on the card, the children may then change to another room if they choose to do so.

The old fashioned infant school timetable, divided into periods of a quarter of an hour for each subject, was based on the premise that 'little children cannot concentrate for longer than this'. The young child however concentrates well for extremely long periods when he is engaged in his own spontaneous activity. In our school, the children are happy and friendly in their approach to adults because they know they are respected and really do matter. It is a child centred environment and we feel that here, where they are not conditioned to dividing their experiences into prescribed subjects, the children not only use their intellect but are bringing their sensitivity to bear to try to understand the many messages in any situation. We hope that when, for example, they are learning about ice and snow, frost and freezing in a situation which is real and involves all their senses, they will at the same time notice the subtle gold, pink, blue and mauve tones when the sun shines on a snowy scene, hear the sound of snow as it slumps off a roof and enjoy the moment of suspense as it is poised curled before it falls.

CHAPTER SIX

Continuity— The junior school

The children in the school are aged between seven and eleven years. They all live in the same community but come from different home backgrounds and they have all shared similar experiences during the first few years of their school lives although their reactions to these experiences may have been very different. The infant school has a similar environment to the one which they are entering in the junior school and the philosophy is basically the same. Most of the children have been eagerly looking forward to the day when they will move to the junior school and great care over a long period has been taken to prepare them for this. Visits to the junior school have been going on all through their infant school life. With the teachers, they have attended dress rehearsals of nativity plays, musical concerts, plays and operettas. Visiting in this way gives them a strong feeling of security and together with the excitement and enjoyment of the entertainment, makes these visits memorable and valuable occasions. Often, they have enjoyed exhibitions of art and craft, they have had the experience of visiting the plant house, seeing the animals, the aviary and the aquarium and are used to visiting the classrooms to see the older children working. Gradually, they have found their way around, become familiar with the atmosphere of the school and the environment in which their older brothers, sisters and friends are living happily. They have learnt the situation of various classes, the teachers' names and have began to develop certain ambitions about the kinds of interesting experiences with which they will want to become involved when they really join the junior school. Some of these interests are noted whilst they are still in the infant school; particularly with regard to the desire to play musical instruments such as recorders, violins, woodwind or brass. When infant children bring messages to teachers or children in the junior school, they may stand and watch lessons taking place in the hall or stop to talk with a brother, sister or friend and follow them into the classroom. The teacher is not surprised to find a young child in her room and will give a friendly word to them. She will not interfere unless she thinks the visit is too long. This is a necessary part of the integration between the two schools.

In a situation where the infant school does not share the same philosophy as the junior school and the children have been used to a formal approach, the settling down period will be much longer. Upon transfer to the progressive junior school from a formal infant school, the children must be given time to reorientate themselves and enjoy the newly found freedom. Some children will wait for direction and instruction and may be unable to choose an activity for themselves whilst others will use their freedom outside the bounds of acceptable behaviour. Slowly, by trial and error on the part of the children, by much patience and kindness on the part of the teacher and as the children become absorbed in the interests and in the wide area of interests covered by the new environment, the children become adjusted. Where progressive methods are used in both the infant and junior schools, children soon recognize that their new society consists largely of older and more mature children. The purpose and pattern of life is similar to that of the infant school and this bolsters the child's confidence and security. The school is child centred and is based on standards which are natural and attainable by children and not on imposed adult standards which have the effect of inhibiting the children.

On the first day of the Autumn term, the children go to the infant school as usual, assemble in a familiar group and are welcomed by their teacher. During the first hour of the morning, the junior school teacher arrives to take her eighteen or more new children to their room in the junior school. They have spent most of their infant school lives together in a family grouped class and it gives them added security to remain together for this difficult transition. It is only occasionally that it becomes necessary to alter the make-up of the groups. However carefully the two schools ease the transfer for the children, there may be unavoidable pressures which must be considered. An older junior school child may perpetuate the myth to the younger child that the teachers are very strict in the junior school or 'You get the cane if you're naughty'. The fears thus established can only be allayed by the teacher's demonstration of fairmindedness and her careful handling of any delicate situations which may arise. A family group of infant children will arrive and join a class in which there are already approximately twenty second-year children who have spent a year in the same room with the same teacher. Many of them will have already been in the same class as the new children whilst they were in the infant school. They will welcome the new members of their class and look after their immediate needs, such as finding them a place in the cloakroom, taking them along to morning assembly. In the classroom, they will introduce them to some of the interesting situations and materials and become involved in interests with them. The two groups of children become united and learning situations common to both develop. In a vertically grouped class, the teacher has the advantage of knowing half the class, having taught them for the previous year. She knows their different personalities and characters and their various home circumstances. She has met the parents on many occasions and feels very close to the family and the child and will have developed a feeling of respect between herself and the home. She knows the stages which the child has reached in concept development, the child's ability in reading and comprehension and how he expresses himself in written and spoken language and creatively. She will be able to turn her attention to the first-year children with far more freedom than if the whole of her class were new to her. She will already have gained a considerable amount of information about them through her discussions with the infant teachers. She is able to refer to the records which have been passed on to her and can discuss the children with their previous teacher whenever necessary during the year. In the third- and fourth-year vertically grouped classes there is the added advantage that the children's previous teacher is in the school and can be referred to even more easily.

A visitor to the school will first find himself in the foyer which is the hub of the school. Every member of the school must pass through the foyer many times during a day. It is in this focal point that the school library is situated. Throughout the day, one of the four child librarians will be on duty to supervise the library. He will often help the younger children to find information from reference books and explain the methods for this. It is in this central position that the filmstrips and other visual aids are kept and the teachers have a separate shelf for their own reference books. This week the book display in a corner of the library is about animals. Helen, who is looking at a book about dogs, explains that this particular book caught her eye as she was passing through the library and as she recently acquired a puppy for her birthday, she is eager to learn more about how to look after her pet. Colin, a bright ten-year-old is sitting at a table and is surrounded by maps. He has planned the route to Gorleston and he will recommend this route to his father when the family go there at half-term. He has drawn a map showing the route, worked out the mileage, the petrol consumption and the estimated time for the journey and is now preparing the driver's route showing towns, large villages and road numbers. He has employed a similar style to that used by the AA and RAC. After half-term, he explains, he will write a story about his adventures. As the teacher talks with him about the foreign shipping using the nearby port of Great Yarmouth, he becomes really interested and he starts to look at the geographical position of Great Yarmouth in relation to the Continent and soon he is discussing North Sea gas with two other boys. Eileen, who is eight, and a friend are using the card index to find all the books containing information about tea. Other children are exchanging their library books and others are browsing round the shelves searching for information. The library is well used and many of the children have developed a good habit of referring to books. When the school library proves to be inadequate, the children walk to the local branch of the County Library which is in a separate building on the same site. The school library is classified by a modified form of the Dewey System of Classification so that usually the children know the classification number of the book they want because of the search they have already made in the school library. In cases of difficulty however the librarian on duty is always helpful and often orders a book from the County Library Headquarters if it is not immediately available. Topic sets of books are also ordered from the County Library for the teachers. The work for the teacher responsible for running the school library is time-consuming but interesting and rewarding. David has chosen a book on light and has taken it back to the activity space leading off from the hall. He has become involved with a friend working with suggestions from this book and the children are now trying to catch the sun's rays in a lens which is directed into a mirror. The experiment is a delicate one and they continue to arrange the apparatus, searching for a satisfactory result. At the other end of the bench, a group of boys are putting the finishing touches to a four feet long model of the Q4 liner. They have collected all the possible information about this new ship from newspapers and magazines and have compiled an interesting illustrated book with plans, maps and drawings. The classroom to which these children belong is transformed into a travel bureau. The interest started when five boys and girls began writing to coastal resorts for brochures. The prompt replies were so encouraging that they wrote to other towns. The children began recording their replies by pinning flags on a map of the British Isles. They obtained brochures from holiday camps and timetables from bus companies, British Rail and the local airport. Inquiry forms were duplicated and any member of the class can now inquire about the possibility of spending a holiday in a particular resort. They will receive carefully worked out information about travel, accommodation, amenities and places of interest around the resort. Children from other classes have been invited to take part and most of the classes are now involved. Inquiries are scrutinized and records kept about types of travel and preferences for different types of accommodation. The popularity of caravans, boarding-houses, holiday camps and of various resorts is obvious from the diagrammatic, pictorial and statistical recording. The number of brochures which are taken home for parents to see and the fact that the charge of 4d does not deter children, points to the possibility that many of the inquiries are serious.

Another continuous interest throughout the school is the production of the school newspaper. There is never any shortage of material and in the room we are visiting children are busy working on articles, poems and stories. A team captain is preparing a report of the recent football match, a librarian is listing the titles of new books in the library and a club secretary is writing an account of their club activities. The class reporter is preparing an account of the class visit to York to add to other items of class news which might be of interest to the rest of the school. Competitions, crossword puzzles, riddles, jokes and illustrations are also part of the school newspaper and one popular competition involves the writing of the next chapter for a serial story. This attracts dozens of entries. The income from the sale of the newspaper which is usually 1d per copy is used to buy book tokens for the winners of competitions. A small committee of children helps the teacher to select the material and makes suggestions for improving the publication.

In one class of third- and fourth-year children, a corner of the room is darkened by a temporary hessian screen hanging from the ceiling and the projector is in use. Four children are being directed by their teacher's voice on a tape recorder:

> Now we will look at slide number 16.
>
> This photograph of the River Aire is taken only half a mile from the point where it emerges from the hillside. It has already flowed many miles underground from its source.
>
> This is a good position for you to look for fish, plant life and water creatures and to take the temperature, note whether the water is slow or fast flowing and discover if the water is soft or hard.
>
> The shape and structure of the bridge is interesting. You will be able to discover the material which was used to build it and give reasons for its shape and strength.
>
> When you have finished looking at the slide and making notes, you can switch on the tape recorder again.
>
> Switch off now.

These children are preparing for a visit to Malham in Yorkshire where they will spend one week. They read information, draw maps, discuss and make apparatus ready for this field expedition. By working in this way in small groups, they are also prepared socially and emotionally for the experience of being away from home for the first time. When they are in Malham this carries over into a feeling of security in each other.

Some school visits may be of shorter duration, perhaps an afternoon or a day spent in visiting local places of interest. Some visits may be of a week's duration at home or abroad. In the Midlands, a radius of 100 to 120 miles gives ample scope and possibilities for day visits. It is important for the younger children to get used to making short expeditions with their teacher. Class 6 have made a visit once a fortnight throughout the past year to observe a nearby pond which is within easy walking distance of the school and were delighted to return yesterday with the biggest newt of the season. These visits are valuable educationally but also help as a preparation for visits farther afield. The conversations during these visits are recorded on portable tape-recorders and as we listen to one of these tapes played back, made when the children visited Coventry Cathedral, we hear Carol say to her teacher: 'It's so beautiful, it makes me want to cry.' On recording another occasion, when the class were walking on the Dover dockside to board a cross channel ferry, a boy's voice, suitably dramatic, is heard to say: 'This must be the biggest thing in the world.' There is a recording of a Beefeater at the Tower of London describing some of the horrors of the Fire of London and the Plague. Brian became so absorbed in the story that he was reliving the situation and we hear him ask: 'And did all my friends escape as well as me?'

Class 9 visited London last week and in their room some children are working at topics which have arisen from the visit. The Crown Jewels are being modelled in clay and other children are doing research into the origin of the various treasures which involves history and geography. A keen interest in photography has developed and is being used to help in realistic picture making and the building of models. In the next first- and second-year vertically grouped class we visit the pattern is similar. Some children are working or discussing in small groups whilst others are working by themselves and seem oblivious of the various activities which are taking place around them. Out on the terrace Helen is painting at an easel and she explains to us that her picture of a donkey, a dog and two children climbing up a rough path on a mountainside is a scene to illustrate the story which she has just completed. Two other children are working with a variety of prisms and optical lenses. They have already discovered that the prism breaks up white light into spectrum colours. They are now experimenting with the various distances they can hold the prism from the wall to match two images or make the images appear in symmetry. The method of the experiment is conducted in a highly scientific manner and the information is all being recorded and measured. The woodwork bench is outside too and four children are using more advanced tools in a more highly skilled way than they did in earlier school life. One boy is making a rope ladder for his model of a castle, illustrating one method of scaling a castle wall. Another boy is chipping at a piece of wood which he found on the river bank yesterday when his class went on a nature expedition. His task seems formidable. He intends to shape the wood into a totem pole similar to one which he saw in the local museum a few weeks ago. He is using a penknife, two files and a screwdriver which he is using as a chisel. A girl who is making an aeroplane out of wood is enjoying this work and it seems that she is doing this as her contribution to a project on transport. Around the next corner a child is sitting in the sun engrossed in a book of adventure stories. On the grass two children are discussing the script of a play to perform with the puppets they have just finished. Some distance away, a group of children are trying to work out the height of an apple tree which is too high for them to reach up to measure. These calculations are involved but they seem to know what they are doing.

In another class the teacher is sitting with Jill in the corner of the room devoted mainly to maths and they are working with Dienes MAB material. Apparently Jill ran into difficulty in giving the correct change in the shop this morning and the teacher is reminding her of an earlier experience with mixed bases. Heather came into school this morning and announced that it was Daddy's birthday and that he was thirty-six. The children started to discuss and compare ages. They began setting problems such as how many of their ages it would take to be added together to make Heather's Daddy's age, how long his schooldays were, how long he had been in the Forces and so on. One child was intrigued by the alternate odd and even numerical value of birthdays. Thirty-six became a fascinating number for this group of children and they began to work out in abstraction with only occasional reference to concrete materials all the possible combinations of amounts making thirty-six which they called 'The Story of Thirty-Six'.

The milliner's shop stocks a variety of hats which have been made by the children and here Jane is adding up the takings. She is counting the money and comparing the answer with her calculation on paper. In a vertically grouped class, to cover the needs of every child, the maximum range of mathematical materials must be provided. In the first class, there may be one or two children who are still developing an understanding of one to one correspondence and notation and at the other end of the scale there will be some who are making good progress in algebra or geometry. In practice, and by allowing a child to choose his activity, vertical grouping leads to an economy in materials. For example, if the school uses Dienes MAB material, one set is enough for each class.

As we move on round the school we see a teacher and four children emptying the kiln. They discuss each piece of fired claywork as it appears and the teacher talks about biscuit firing and explains about the colouring and glazing processes which will follow. Behind this group, two boys on a stepladder are working out a pulley system to raise a bucket containing sand. When we ask for an explanation, they talk about their experiments where they are using varied amounts of sand and a varied number of pulleys as a progression of work on levers which they were doing last week. These boys have developed quite a scientific attitude to their work and are not disheartened when an experiment fails. In the next classroom, it is immediately obvious that the teacher's own interest in art has influenced the children. The booklets produced by the children are decorated artistically. The nature corner and a display of pottery are most attractively arranged and backed by printed fabric and in the library corner there is a flowering plant on the low table. A mobile made of spiral wood shavings is hanging from the middle of the ceiling. Two children using a simple slide rule are checking their answers on a desk calculator. Another child is following a programme on the multiplication of fractions on the teaching machine. Mark is tapping out a story on an old typewriter. Graham who is the announcer and compère for a class magazine which has been recorded on tape is making notes as he listens to the playback of the tape. The magazine will then be rerecorded onto another tape recorder and he will fit his script in between the items. On the science bench, two boys have fixed a light on to the lighthouse they have made and are having difficulty in working out a method of making the light flash on and off. None of their attempts has so far been successful. Class wall newspapers or newsboards are a feature of this classroom. These are used in the same way and for the same purpose as the school newspaper and this gives more children in the class the opportunity to contribute. The children soon develop the habit of looking at the newspaper at home and bringing interesting news items to school. An interest in local, national or international news will often lead to a serious study of the situation. Amongst the most successful of these in the past have been happenings which have aroused the children's feelings of sympathy or pity; feelings of anger, hate or fear; of adventure and discovery. The Suez crisis, the Middle East war, the assassination of President Kennedy, the Munich air crash, the Torrey Canyon shipwreck, the drilling for North Sea gas, Sir Francis Chichester's voyage round the world, royal visits to other countries, civil wars, race riots, volcanic eruptions, earthquakes, floods, tornadoes formed some of the topics. Children produce reported accounts and sometimes write as if they have taken part themselves. They illustrate their stories by pictures, drawings and maps and bind them together in book form.

A television room in the school would be ideal but this facility is not available and so we use part of the foyer. All television broadcasts suitable for juniors are available to the children. Each class has a timetable of programmes and the teachers remind the children of the times of the programmes for which they might have been waiting. Some watch because of the bearing which the programme has on the work in hand. Others watch because of a genuine interest in the subject and others just out of curiosity. Such programmes as the State Opening of Parliament or the Trooping of the Colour are very popular and then suitable arrangements are made to accommodate a large number of children. Some of the wireless programmes are of interest to only a few children and in this case, the classroom loudspeaker or a transistor radio can be situated in a corner of the classroom with the volume turned down, but children often use the staffroom if it is available.

In the PE lesson in progress in the hall the teacher has begun by suggesting to the children that they are being slowly wound up like a spring. The children have used their imagination and have adopted various positions. Some have wound themselves up on the floor like a clock spring, others have sunk lower and lower on to their toes and have curled up into a ball like a bed spring. Some girls have fallen over backwards making an arch with only their toes and hands touching the ground. A boy is leaning as far forward as he can without losing his balance, another stretching as high as he can into the air with the tension of a stretched spring. 'Tighter, tighter,' says the teacher. 'Hold it, we are going to release the tension, now!' The motionless bodies spring into action and the hall is filled with children turning, twisting, rolling and stretching. Some are intricate movements, others are more simple but all the children are giving their own individual interpretation of the feeling and at the end the children lie relaxed on the floor. When this class has left the hall is soon occupied by two groups of children who want to develop two dramatic situations. Ten minutes later, at one end of the hall, firemen are fighting a fire and a poor woman clutching a doll as a baby is crying: 'I've saved my baby.' From her intonation the audience knows that the baby is really dead. Another woman comforts her as the ambulance arrives. At the other end of the hall, a prisoner attended by a policeman is on trial for theft. The judge is sitting high up on some stage blocks, the barristers face him from the floor, witnesses are sitting behind them and on one side are twelve chairs for the jury but only a few are occupied. In both these situations, the principal characters are dressed up and all the children are really living the part. The teacher supervising these activities has decided to help the trial which is proceeding particularly well by bringing the rest of the class into the public gallery at the end of the afternoon and to fill the empty jury chairs. During the last twenty minutes of the day, the trial will be repeated in its entirety.

We can hear music and in the next room we find a Carl Orff type lesson in progress where many of the Studio 49 instruments are being used. There is one large base xylophone, two or three tenor xylophones as well as alto and treble xylophones. There are descant and alto glockenspiels, timpani and tambourines. These are supplemented by violins, 'cellos, guitars, a zither, a mandolin, a bass and side drums and other percussion instruments. The group is composing a tune which is being played in four parts and there is tremendous concentration on the part of all the children. There is always the opportunity for any child to learn and to play any orchestral instrument but this type of lesson arouses interest in those children who have not yet shown any marked ability or joined an orchestral group. The viola is a restrung violin and one child is learning to play a string bass. The wind section includes cornets, trumpets, trombones, flutes, clarinets and saxophones. These groups meet with a teacher after school or at dinner times and they receive further instruction from a peripatetic music specialist who visits the school each week. Many children play a recorder, either a soprano, descant, treble, tenor or bass and some older children are able to play more than one of these. The junior and senior choirs which meet regularly after school complete the range of the musical life of the school. Some of the more talented musicians spend Saturday mornings at the County School of Music where they receive further instruction and a few children play in the County Junior Orchestra.

If we follow the group of children who are walking through the foyer we shall arrive at the caravan which is in the charge of a teacher who has specialist knowledge of the problems of the maladjusted child and those who are slow to learn. Similar small groups visit the caravan throughout the day and the children enjoy working with the interesting apparatus and activities. As well as reading masters, teaching machines and transistor tape recorders, there are quantities of interesting materials. The children have a very close and intimate contact with the teacher. She hears about their difficulties and is able to help with emotional problems and anxieties and tries to give them a stronger feeling of security. The class teacher works in close relationship with this specialist teacher and reinforces her work.

The learning of French is concentrated in conversation which helps the children to build up structures and vocabulary. Playing games and singing songs also helps. The children use records and make tape recordings themselves which are sometimes the background for a series of lessons. The tape recorder is used to help children with pronunciation and accent. The teachers have devised their method of teaching through experience and have adapted the best features of all the published material and together with their own good accents, fluent command of the language, enthusiasm and ability, the lessons are really enjoyed by the children.

An attempt is made to use the interests and special abilities of every member of the staff to the best advantage for the school. Three teachers make special contributions to the musical life of the school. Besides teaching and encouraging children to make music, they arrange musical evenings when about half the children in the school take part. These teachers produce operettas, carol services and nativity plays in conjunction with the teachers who take an interest in dramatic work and dance. Occasionally, the music teachers arrange an evening concert as an entertainment for the children and their parents. On these evenings the teachers invite guest artists from the senior County Orchestra to perform with them. Teachers and children make contributions towards the presentation of any performance by designing and painting scenery, making properties and costumes, etc. The untimetabled day allows freedom for these things to be developed. Some teachers devote many hours after school and give up their Saturday mornings to training the football, swimming, cricket, netball and athletic teams and others hold country dance and square dancing sessions after school. Chess and stamp collecting clubs are popular and plans are being made for a sailing and canoeing club. One teacher is especially interested in the electrical equipment of the school and combines this with photography. He is responsible for the different projectors and cameras, the tape recorders, record players and the television and radio sets. Other members of the staff consult him when they need advice or assistance and he orders films, filmstrips and records for them. This interest in audio and visual aids covers the ordering and distribution of specimens and models made available to schools by the Leicester Museum. Another teacher makes his knowledge of animals and aquaria available to the rest of the staff and is responsible for the animal house, aviary and plant house. Flowers and house plants are always available for the classrooms and children are able to grow their own specimens in ideal conditions. Other teachers have special knowledge and experience in environmental study, natural history, sewing, pottery, puppetry and flower arranging. Small exhibitions of children's work are arranged and occasionally a much larger one of work in art and craft is held to which parents are invited. One teacher is responsible for integrating the maths and English teaching in the school. His services are particularly useful when newly qualified teachers are appointed. In these ways the teachers are able to help each other. If particular knowledge and experience is required which is not available in the school, the county advisory staff is always ready to help.

On Friday evenings, the staff meet socially in the school for swimming, badminton, table tennis and bridge and bring their friends, husbands or wives. These evenings are very popular and help the newly qualified teachers to adjust and to settle in to a district which may be new to them and where they may not yet have made any friends. These meetings are indicative of the integration and happiness of life within the school which is made as rich and interesting as possible with opportunities provided for every child and adult to take an active part and make their own individual contribution.

CHAPTER SEVEN

A quintet

Space does not permit the inclusion of the records of all the children in the school so five children have been chosen as a small cross-section of the school population. From the cumulative records of these five children, the most relevant points have been extracted. It must be stressed that these are only the bare bones of the records showing the development of the children.

The time is 1.00 pm on a fine January day. In the junior school, lunch has just finished and the children are dispersing. Some go out into the grounds of the school and some to the library. A group of children are rehearsing a play in one room and in another, a dozen children are working out ideas for the school assembly which is to be held on the following day. Children have returned to several rooms to continue with pieces of urgent work and in one room, Jean and Margaret are helping a teacher to clear out a storeroom. In one classroom, six children are waiting for a teacher to arrive to help them practise their particular piece for the forthcoming musical evening. All of these children are learning to play the violin. While they wait, one girl, Pat, has taken over the role of the teacher and the minuet which they are playing is frequently interrupted by Pat's instructions. Pat is the first member of the quintet.

In a far corner of the hall, David is practising on the oboe. This is another member of the quintet. David, a serious-faced boy with an intent expression in his eyes, is conscientious and tenacious in all that he does and shows considerable artistic flair.

A teacher is talking with a dozen of the junior recorder group in the foyer. These twelve children are all first- or second-year children who are learning to play the descant recorder as an introduction to making music for themselves. Some are already proficient but some appear to be experiencing difficulties. One of these is a dark-haired girl who wears glasses. She is dressed in a thin summer

Two top junior girls using the large easels which have special boxes fitted to them to hold pots of paint and water.

A group of boys putting the finishing touches to a large model of the *Queen Elizabeth II* they have built together.

frock worn over a jumper. This is Joan, the third in the quintet.

Charles is a 'cello player. Over by the tank of terrapins, Charles is leaning on his 'cello case. This boy, who is in the fourth year of the junior school, has considerable musical ability but appears to approach this and other children without enthusiasm. Charles will spend the whole of lunchtime standing there unless a teacher hustles him away into doing something else. He chats to passers by and pesters any teacher he sees to give him 'a job'. This is his ruse to inveigle an adult into a long conversation. Charles is both irritating and disarming and is spoken of in the staffroom with an affectionate shudder.

Doreen is the last member of the quintet. She seems a shy tentative child who rarely ventures any comment. Doreen's one real enthusiasm is the rhythmical expression involved in Carl Orff music and she is a member of the percussion section of the school orchestra.

PAT
Date of birth 29th August 1957, position in family 1/2.
Autumn term 1962
Pat is a week late starting school as the family have only recently moved to the district. Mother brought her. Pat left her mother easily and confidently.

Confident and eager to join in everything. Within a week has tried most things in the room but tendency to steer away from water and sand. Occasionally spends brief periods here but never gets really involved.

Had a setback today. Frightened by an older boy on the way to school. Wept.

Signs of disturbance for several days.

Things more adjusted again – got over her upset. Loves to confide items of personal news. A friendly but quiet attitude to me.

Went to the sand-tray this morning. I joined her and encouraged her to get more deeply involved.

Parents' interview – mother and father attended, had obtained a baby sitter. Very interested to know about 'new methods'. Pat a happy child at home too. Appear to be no real problems. Parents keen to understand and cooperate with school.

Brought a Christmas tree and trimmings for the room and a large bag of sweets to be shared between the children. Rather shy at the party and obviously very concerned with being polite.

Spring term 1963
Had a Post Office for Christmas and brought it to school. Gave me a letter but when I opened it, it said: 'Dear Pat, I love you, from Daddy' – obviously the wrong letter. She is both loved and loving.

Is growing her hair into pigtails she says.

Extremely interested in books and is really beginning to read. She has an intelligent approach – guesses a lot of words but employs look and say and context mainly. Will read her way steadily through a shelf of books.

Language and use of materials show that she is very aware of size and shape. Can count and count in groups.

Drawings very advanced – dressed in clothes and very realistic.

Understands and uses the correct terms for equality and inequality. Understands conservation of number.

Summer term 1963
Mother reported to be having a baby.

Enjoys movement and PE.

Reading well and expressively and with comprehension using the phonetic sounds of letters to help with new words. Much of her reading is silent. I checked today to see how many sounds she knew. She was quite puzzled by this at first and I thought I might have done the wrong thing but she is well aware of them all. Came a little later on to say: 'Sometimes it's two letters that make one sound' and she went through the book *A Little Brown Clock* actually analysing for herself the digraphs, etc.

She has a gentle disposition, an innate willingness to work and is a definite leader in her group.

Louise is her constant companion but although Louise tends to be the follower she seems on the surface to be the more forceful personality. Pat and Louise developed and organized a hat shop with hats made by her and her friends.

Parents' interview. Mother and father attended. Seem very happy about everything in school.

Autumn term 1963
She understands conservation of amount and quantity. She is still using natural units of measurement. Recording number work pictorially.

Pat now has a baby brother and according to the written work in her book, delights in holding and feeding him. Her mother allowed her to do this right from his being a few days old. Pat obviously knows she is trusted and regarded as quite capable.

Played in the house again although had previously abandoned domestic play.

Organized a hospital. Pat the doctor. Kept records including temperature charts. Pat's mother was a nurse and everything most realistic involving lots of maths and science. The hospital has turned into a clinic. Pat is the receptionist and the appointments book is remarkable.

Pat can already tell the time but throughout this period has experimented with 'the passage of time'. She has done a lot of work using the pinger, egg timer and metronome and can judge almost accurately when a certain amount of time has elapsed.

Mother brought baby up to school today. Started to make the second book about her baby brother.

Working with pendulums today. Involved timing devices with the pendulum. Moved into the hall with this interest and is using the climbing frames to get a bigger swing for the pendulums. Has shown ingenuity in devising pendulums.

Frido balls were one of her ideas. With these she could also push pieces of wood into the holes to weight them.

Enjoys PE and dance. Very lithe and understands quality of movement.

Spring term 1964
Keen on art just now. Has spent a long time experimenting with colours. Her paintings are usually scenes, e.g. 'The Bus Stop Queue' or 'My Day at Bradgate Park'. Figures drawn in moving positions.

Interested in music. Can combine various rhythms into a longer piece. Sings in tune and correct notation and understands dynamics. Enjoys listening and making music. Uses the piano quite a lot.

Made a whole new set of clothes for her doll.

I suddenly became aware that Pat is poised and self confident. She is never alone. She is constantly 'doing' and is rarely inactive. Even in discussion times she is alert all the time ready to contribute.

Summer term 1964
Rosemary who lives in the same road has recently joined the class and

Pat is protective towards her. This I feel is a good thing because it is forcing Pat into a slightly slower tempo at times.

Pat uses the tape recorder and typewriter competently. Her use of language is good but is often not so expressive as some of the apparently less able children. Pat's written work is well presented. She uses a wide vocabulary, can write most things for herself and if she does want to know a word, can carry the alphabetical spelling in her mind. She does not however often expose much of her own intimate thoughts and feelings in her writing. This comes out more in spontaneous drama.

She continues to organize groups of children in all kinds of activities.

Pat is now writing story books about characters of her own imagining who are always aptly named. She illustrates them with delightful drawings and the other children are using these books as reading material.

When it is her turn to count the dinner money she is swift and accurate. She is logical and very thorough in any mathematical situation.

She has a good memory and learns poems etc much more quickly than anyone (including me).

Painted a large size Moby Dick.

Showed an interest in clouds yesterday and arrived at school today with lots of information and pictures about clouds. Used reference books for research producing a well planned 'Information Book on Clouds'. Drawings here have shown a grasp of perspective.

Pat, Louise and Mark find the names of all nature specimens and write the labels and help children to read captions round the room. They often read to children and listen to children reading.

I asked what she enjoyed best. She said reading. She is a keen and fluent reader and really addicted to books.

Has started a portrait gallery of the class and is obtaining some remarkable likenesses. Her sense of humour shows here and the other children seem to enjoy her exaggeration of some of their peculiarities.

Tommy who has sandy freckles all over his face was not at all dismayed when Pat exaggerated these. Much of this tolerance is due to Pat's handling of the situation.

Just lately, although feeling that Pat still works well, she seems to want recognition all the time. I discussed this with her mother who agrees that this is also so at home. She has two younger brothers, one who has just started school and the other who is now beginning to move around and to chatter. Perhaps this is the reason.

Pat's stories have now become schoolgirl adventures. Her reading matter at home has obviously changed to books about girls at boarding-school.

The Roneo machine has been standing idle for some time so I have suggested to the Pat, Louise and Mark group that they should edit and print a newspaper. This has enthused her and there are reporters, copywriters and printers. Pat of course is the editor. She is recognized as the most able and there seem no feelings of jealousy.

I noticed that when the children were playing at sports the other day Pat could not jump very high, but she still went on with the game and showed no signs of disappointment. She just accepted the fact that although she excels in many things, in this she doesn't.

She has been one of the natural leaders in the group but I have never overstressed this (at least not consciously).

Pat is extremely well informed both from her conversation with adults and from books and this to some extent seems to have dulled her desire to experiment and discover.

Very confident about her transfer to the junior school. During her time with us she has had no absences and parents have attended all six arranged interviews as well as every open evening and school function.

Transfer to junior school.

Autumn term 1964
Brought a letter from mother on the first morning asking if Pat could have violin lessons. Checked with infant school about musical ability. During first week is given instrument and has first lesson.

Has settled down very quickly in class and has written a long account of her summer holiday.

Paints excellent imaginative pictures and gets deeply involved in dramatic situations.

Has brought clothes for the dressing up box from home.

Tends to mix more with the older children in the class.

Has joined the first-year descant recorder group.

Has been rather withdrawn this week although her work has been good.

Painted a picture of Mother taking baby in the pram to see the doctor.

Spring term 1965
The music teacher has picked Pat out as a talented child. Often to be seen listening to the senior orchestra practising. Has joined the second-year recorder goup.

Frequent visitor to the school library. Takes other children and finds books for them. Avid reader. Always has a library book in her violin case. Reads schoolgirl stories and books about animals.

Brought a collection of twigs from dormant trees already identified and labelled. Arranged them in nature corner.

After seeing *Alice in Wonderland* presented by the visiting drama group, Pat and a group of children produced the children's interpretation of this. Pat was Alice. Read the story. All her work connected with Alice this week. Made a model stage with cardboard characters.

Wrote a mathematical story about doing the weekly shopping involving buying food on Saturday morning and going to town in the afternoon to buy shoes and baby clothes ready for the winter.

Pat is being taught to play chess by a second-year boy. She never lets him forget her daily game.

During the last three weeks Pat's day has been devoted to maths, story writing and collage work.

The teacher of French remarks on Pat's good memory for vocabulary as well as her good accent.

Pat has a keen but quiet sense of humour.

Summer term 1965
All teachers who come into contact with Pat remark on her personality, her qualities of leadership and her eagerness and ability to involve herself in learning situations.

Absent from school suffering from a cold. Mother comes up to school for her library books and brought a letter from Pat to her friend.

Wants to stay to lunch so that she can join the junior orchestra which practises at lunchtimes.

Obviously mathematically aware. Enjoys bringing mathematics into all her work.

Brought money for the swimming pool fund raised by holding a bring-and-buy sale in her garden.

Started to write a collection of stories which she can read to her brother at bedtime. The main character is Pongo, a kindly gonk who does good deeds.

At parents' interview anxious to discover if parents were exerting pressure on Pat. Found them to be very sensible in their attitude. Father a foreman in an engineering works. Seem unaware of Pat's real ability.

Autumn term 1965
Pat is enjoying mothering the new first-year children, helping them to settle down and helping to introduce them to interesting situations in the room.

The music teacher has accepted her into the treble recorder group.

Swam today for the first time – 'I could nearly swim last term.'

Organized a group of children in her class to take morning assembly. Service started with a short play about a mother and father putting their three children to bed and singing 'Golden Slumbers' as a lullaby. The hymn chosen was 'Morning has broken' and the prayer which Pat said had been written by her.

The nights are short,
The days are long.
A good night's sleep
Makes us strong.
It rests our limbs,
It rests our brain,
It rests our eyes
And heals our pain
When we see daylight through the curtain creep,
We thank you, God, for a good night's sleep.

Pat has become deeply involved in studying ancient number systems and calculating devices. David has been brought in by her to help. She is writing a book on this subject. Wants to tell the rest of the class about this when she has finished. Large diagrams are being prepared by her 'so that they can all see'.

Reads lots of books during a week, attends orchestra, choir and recorder practices once a week; is a member of the nature club. Time is fully occupied.

Spring term 1966
Has asked to be a librarian in the school library.
 Taking her responsibilities very seriously. Arrives at school early to arrange the library for the day ahead and has also undertaken the organization of book displays.
 In nature study she has become interested in the human body, skeleton, nervous system, etc.
 She is now conducting a survey of all the children in the school to find out the rate of human growth from birth. Her inquiry form asks for weight and length at birth and present age, weight and height. She has produced graphs and a book on this subject. Throughout this investigation Pat has avoided all mention of reproduction and birth. This seems to worry her. After consulting her mother it was decided to give her a book on this subject suitable for her age.
 A normal pattern of behaviour has again emerged which seems to indicate her acceptance of the facts of life as presented to her by the book and simple explanations by her mother.

Summer term 1966
There is a possibility that Pat might be considered for transfer to the high school at the end of her third year when she is ten years of age.
 Mother hopes to take up part time employment soon.
 Pat takes the move to a third- and fourth-year class in her stride.
 She has begun to write plays although so far none have been performed. Recently, the most interesting of these was about a seven-year-old West Indian boy who came to live in England and was the only coloured boy. An older girl (no doubt Pat) protected him and taught him English.
 Pat was chosen to take the place of a librarian who was absent. Enjoys this experience and was knowledgeable about the library routine.

Autumn term 1966
Visited Church Langton in south Leicestershire for a week with her class on a field study course. First experience of being away from home. Pat was not homesick. Her attention attracted by water life. Arrived armed with test tubes, a bottle of alcohol and a large magnifying glass. Worked scientifically.

Spring term 1967
In mathematics today did work involving fractions and decimals. Wrote the outline of the nativity play for Christmas which was performed at the parents' Carol Service.

Joined a small group of children who are conducting a survey of the trees growing in the village. After the weekend Pat supplied a great amount of information for this.

Summer term 1967
Now attends County Junior Orchestra on Saturday mornings; playing violin very well. Practises at home.

At a staff meeting the possibility of transferring Pat to the high school with the fourth-year children was considered. Things considered were not only her intelligence, academic ability, knowledge and experience, but her physical maturity, emotional stability and the fact that most of her friends were fourth-year children. They all felt that she would benefit earlier than most children from the more mature school environment of the high school.

DAVID
Date of birth 4th February 1957, position in family 2/2.

Summer term 1962
David was solemn for the first few days but showed no outward signs of distress. He is quiet and deliberate in his movements and in his speech. Everything is worked through slowly but systematically and thoroughly. When he has to go anywhere he moves in a direct line purposefully.

His main interest is drawing with crayon. The pictures he produces are usually of houses or buses firmly drawn and symmetrical.

He does not appear to need other children's friendship but is always polite to them.

Very well cared for. Works alone. Fascinated by the guinea-pig.

David spends a long time working something out, thoughtfully turning something over in his hands or perhaps holding it up to the light, examining and testing.

Graham has produced a film of our museum visit and David volunteered to turn the handle. He puts out no feelers for friendship but is not negative to other children. He has a sort of contained openness in his make-up.

Autumn term 1962
Watching Barbara with the guinea-pig today and obviously feeling that perhaps the guinea-pig was being held too closely, he tapped Barbara on the shoulder and said 'Watch out, she'll smothercate.'

Enjoys time outside during this sunny weather. Has been fascinated by shadows.

Searching for insects today, turned over a stone, stood watching the insects for a while, decided which he needed to gather and skilfully and deliberately collected them. He uses his hands gently but is very sure. He also returned the insects to their original place after he had finished observing, sketching and comparing them and they were none the worse.

David finds the mechanics of writing easy. He has excellent kinaesthetic control. He does not talk a lot about his experiences and drawing seems to be a satisfactory mode of expression for him at the moment. Paints every day. Spends at least half an hour on one painting.

Is forming a firm friendship with Stephen and Keith. They now work together on junk work. David however is not satisfied with crude representation as are the other two. For him the model must be realistic. He is adept at handling materials and copes with small fiddly things such as putting a paper clip through a wheel and bending it back. He told me that he worked a lot with meccano at home.

Talking more. Offers thoughtful comments during discussion.

Always sits upright with both feet firmly planted on the floor.

Attacks PE climbing apparatus in the same slow but deliberate way. Natural movements tend to be slow and sustained, quite unusual for such a young boy.

David is very popular with his fellows and attempts are made to include him in most ventures. David sometimes declines.

Parents' interview. Mother attended. Spoke of how quiet and distant he seemed at home. Certainly, nothing seems to excite or hurry him. Perhaps I should say he doesn't show excitement as the other children do. He has a serious attitude to his work, perseveres and sees it through to a finish no matter how difficult and he does experience considerable difficulty at times.

Spring term 1963
The trio David, Stephen and Keith are now firm friends. They spend a lot of time with the animals, the guinea-pig and the gerbils, not just holding them or touching but really observing, imagining and making mazes, houses out of bricks, tunnels and all kinds of different environments particularly for the gerbils.

Talking more and descriptively, I have transcribed some of his conversation. He enjoys copying and illustrating it. Presentation good.

David enjoys manipulating clay and sand as opposed to 'making' things. He helped to create sand landscapes and painted a picture of them afterwards.

Enjoys work with the sorting and grouping box and, being David, is insisting on working steadily through the books which are supplied with it.

David really thinks about things and is attentive but is never quick off the mark with anything.

He is beginning to show an interest in reading and is spending more time in the book corner. Stephen reads fluently and David leans over and follows the words as Stephen reads.

A subtle sense of humour. I can now determine times when David is excited by something. His eyes open wider and he extends and closes his fingers but even then his approach is considered and deliberate.

Summer term 1963
Whenever a piece of junk is brought in David can always see the best use for it. Most of the things he suggests are very appropriate.

Still not really reading, I sense that he is getting anxious. David seems to be a boy who needs an analytical approach almost from the start, so I am working with him now on books which have a more phonetic approach. Does not seem at all worried by the somewhat stilted phrases. Has started a magazine on food.

Building with poleidoblocs today – a magnificent building. Drew it from various elevations. Representation good. Draws what he observes.

Today he built on a mirror and again could reproduce it quite closely in drawing.

The trio made an aerodrome with junk material, with helicopters with blades which really turned, a wind sock, etc. They referred to books.

Continued poleidobloc construction using angled mirrors and then a balance bar.

Autumn term 1963
For almost the first time today David laughed and shouted with excitement. He was working at the water trolley and having fun with some ice cubes, floating them, holding them down and letting them bob up, joining them together and watching them diminish. The frozen hand, made with a rubber glove, caused a riot and David was well in the middle of the fun. The trio now call themselves The Frozen Hand Gang.

Introduced a turntable for David's poleidobloc constructions today. After a while he was using it to make a roundabout but obviously taking great care not to damage or mark the turntable in the process. He covered it with a circle of thick card to which he attached the horses.

Building again. Saw a picture of a pyramid in the entrance hall and determined to build one. He couldn't make it with blocks so resorted to stones and enlisted several other children to help. Finished with six pyramids of varying height. Long discussion involving relative size of base to height.

Parents' evening. Mother comments how he has come out lately. Very pleased that he is now reading well.

Has to visit dentist next week for several extractions.

Writing and spelling for himself is still difficult but he perseveres and sees a piece of work through to a finish.

Had six teeth out. Absent from school.

Spring term 1964
David enjoys painting. Time spent on pictures is now as long as an hour and a half, sometimes more. He has a mature sense of colour and design.

Worked out an elaborate roadway system over chairs and tables today, bridging spaces with pieces of hardboard. It was well worked out with road signs etc. When I asked how I travelled between two points I got a detailed and accurate answer. Unfortunately it couldn't be preserved longer than two days because the chairs had to be moved to clean. Did not take up my suggestion to turn it into a map. Perhaps I am pushing him into pictorial representation when he really wants to handle concrete materials. I may have overdone poleidobloc drawings because of his obvious ability.

Summer term 1964
An interesting conversation as the trio are looking at bubble gum cards of prehistoric animals.
David: 'You know there are really such things as monsters.'
Keith: 'No, you're monster mad.'
David: 'They come alive after things are dead.' (strange reversal here).
Stephen: 'Yeah, that's it.'
David: 'If you keep these cards of monsters, they'll come alive.'
Keith: 'How long have you had them then?'
David: 'Three years.'
Keith: 'How long does it take?'
David: 'Twelve years, just a bit before you have to tear them up.'
Stephen: 'Yeah, that's good.'
They all obviously understood each other.

David brought his father's football medals to school today. The thought of his pending move to the junior school has ellicited this. He is longing to play football. The three boys collected two teams from all our seven-year-old boys and those in other rooms and as we had a student in today I was able to take them out to play. David played 'goalie' between two jumping stands and was delighted. It was terribly hot but they didn't mind. Started an interest book about Leicester City football team.

David shows unusual awareness for words.
The bring-and-buy sale was advertised as a 'Big Sale'. David said: 'Must be a big yacht then.'

Produced very advanced drawings on bits of paper which he passed around the trio with such things as 'Pail-faced Indian' and a drawing of an Indian with a bucket for a face.

Made a horse out of chicken wire and paper. Made the tail and head separately and joined them on expertly.

After singing with the teacher in the next class who has a guitar he came back to school this morning and told me just how an electric guitar works. 'My Dad can play a trumpet,' he said, 'and I am going to learn to play one too.'

Understands conservation of amount, length, weight, volume. Knows money values practically but dislikes recording. Will do so and is conscientious about it but not keen. Reads well but seems to have so many other things he likes to do better.

David took his visits to the junior school with his usual calm serene approach, the same 'contained openness' he showed when he first attended school.

Transfer to junior school.

Autumn term 1964
David is very quiet and does not join in group activities. Rather sullen and evasive when spoken to or questioned about his work: 'It's supposed to be ... but I went wrong ... I might do it again.'

He reads well. Story writing is very factual, no sign of imaginative thought. Maths progressing well. Has a good memory. Quick and accurate in mental addition and subtraction.

Has set up his own shop selling pins, nails, tacks, buttons, paper clips, drawing pins, small coils of wire, hair grips, pegs, etc mostly brought from home. This attracted much attention but he was only interested in serious shoppers and turned the inquisitive children away.

Spring term 1965
Father visited school specially to ask if David could learn to play the recorder.

I find it difficult to make contact with David. He seems to avoid me.

Mother visits school and is quite angry because older boys have waylaid David on the way home. Stated her business and went.

David is writing pages of story – handwriting poor, spelling accurate, content mostly about school. Criticizes other children but does not name them. Can recognize criticism of me in some of his stories. David seems to think that the school environment is 'too young' for him.

Summer term 1965
Does not seem to be working up to his capabilities although trying to

lead him into interesting situations. Is rather stubborn and concentrates on calculation, story writing and reading. Prefers books from school library rather than class library. Spends a great deal of time in school library looking at science books, ignores other children around him. If spoken to by a teacher or librarian returns to his class immediately without comment.

Very concerned about David. An enigmatic character. Still hoping to establish a *rapport* with him.

On parents' evening encouraged parents to talk about David's behaviour at home. He reads, writes and draws and has no friends. Mother is his chief companion, father has to work on many evenings. Father is a consultant engineer. Parents feel David is unhappy in school but are full of praise for my efforts to encourage him. I suggest that a move to another class might help and father mentions one teacher whom David is always talking about.

Autumn term 1965
I sense that David has great potential but I seem unable to stimulate him sufficiently. Moved to Class 8. Follows the same pattern of activity. Maths and a great deal of writing. Written work now about travel and begins to study the universe. Excellent diagrams. Very sceptical about Martians but believes in flying saucers and explains his theory of their origin.

Paints his first picture in this school. Pins it on the wall and labels it with a neat title 'The River Wreake at Ratcliffe'. Paints a series of landscapes of places he has visited with his family at weekends.

Refers to books and dictionary naturally, uses an extensive vocabulary.

Making rapid progress on descant recorder. Music teacher gives him his first lesson on the oboe.

Spring term 1966
Can now play the scale and mother is teaching him to read music at home.

At the end of the fourth term I am at last happy about David's progress and his emotional stability, and I have become resigned to his friendless existence at this stage.

Music teacher says he is progressing well and is confident that he is playing the right instrument.

Summer term 1966
David's first contribution to the school newspaper, a cartoon, is accepted; he waited for my reaction when he handed it in, gave a faint smile and walked away. David bought seven copies of the newspaper when it was published.

Often brings cuttings for wall newspaper. Has been asked to write a play for a group of children making puppets and a theatre. They gave him the names of the characters and he offered them a choice of themes. A very successful group effort – the play was performed for other classes.

Today he brought to school his scrap book of Leicester City Football Club started in the infant school. This is full of newspaper cuttings, charts and photographs and covered the whole season.

Autumn term 1966
David transferred to a third- and fourth-year class with a male teacher. Father visited David when he spent a week at Church Langton on a music course. David immediately packed his bag to go home. Situation handled in a way that saved David from embarrassment and he stayed quite happily for the rest of the week. Has joined County Junior Orchestra. The high school is looking forward to having a keen oboe player and have ordered an instrument for him.

Spring term 1967
Shows ability and interest in all subjects but still works largely on his own. Has produced a very comprehensive book on the Israel-Egypt war. Brings the *Daily Telegraph* to school each morning and reads the latest news. Listens to the BBC hourly news. Enjoys French and science particularly. Has worked with levers and pulleys. Started experiments with vacuums. Asked permission to make ice in the icecream refrigerator. Usually likes to demonstrate an experiment and is always successful in capturing an audience.

Summer term 1967
A student on teaching practice has chosen him for a child study and has spent a few evenings at David's home. No television, reads and writes and paints at home. Sister spends each evening doing homework and reading. Both children very knowledgeable about shrubs, roses and garden flowers. A very happy family attached to

All the classrooms have display areas like this where children's work is always on show. They decide themselves which paintings are worthy of display.

An eight-year-old concentrates on his painting.

each other and very seldom entertain friends. They seem not to need them.

Enjoys working with the SRA Reading Laboratory and has become interested in the early settlement of North America through the laboratory cards.

Outstanding mathematical ability. Is collecting quick methods of calculation and has discovered many for himself e.g. the multiplication of 11 rule.

Autumn term 1967
Each Monday records information regarding plants, trees and wild flowers and brings specimens collected on weekend walks with his family.

David has a studious and academic outlook on life and has developed a personal discipline for study which is unusual in a child of his age.

Parents are very pro-school and support the school in everything. My feeling that they might have doubted the validity of modern educational methods for their son was quite a mistaken one.

JOAN
Date of birth 12th July 1958, position in family 4/6

Autumn term 1963
Elder sister brought Joan on first day as mother was ill. Joan very tearful on first morning. Obviously very unsure where she stands in relation to me. Sidles away from any friendly overtures. Has quite a bad squint. Movement ungainly. Fingers of hands held tensely and are not flexible. Says nothing.

By the end of the first week a passive acceptance of having to come to school. Does not protest but sadly 'lost'. Stands about a lot, always very close to me.

Older sister Betty brings her each morning. I have encouraged her to come in to see Joan during the day. Betty very motherly.

Other children's overtures of friendship towards Joan increased possibly due to extra status from Betty visiting.

Referred for eye test.

Attempts to dress herself but needs help. Enjoys house play – usually plays the baby. Talks with children and sometimes to me now.

Has a limited use of language. Trying to ask whether the sand tray was to go on the veranda this morning, 'nanza' was her word for veranda and the question was a hesitant searching for words accompanied by pointing, waving and patting my arm, 'Sand – take nanza – door.'

She seems quite unselfconscious about this and always tries to make herself understood. Has difficulty in getting words out. Uses signs to indicate needs.

Spring term 1964
Always has a lot of spittle in her mouth which rasps when she speaks. When Joan first came to school she was reasonably clean and well dressed but as the term wears on her appearance becomes less prepossessing with her hair lank and unkempt and she always has a runny nose.

The children have made a few comments about Joan but on the whole she is not shunned by them as less cared for children sometimes are. She is willing to do anything for them, does not appear to take notice of any slights and has a comic element in her personality which she seems to play up for the benefit of the other children. She is quite popular. Joan does not appreciate it when older children try to take care of her now and she can assert her personality stubbornly if she wishes.

Comes into school alone.

Glasses with a patch prescribed. Speech therapist reports no obvious actual defect. She does not need treatment at present, will be seen again later to check but suggest a hearing test.

Joan enjoys cleaning and tidying and washing up jobs and does them very well.

Left handed.

Her drawings are just emerging from the scribble stage and today's drawing of Mummy was a head with eyes, arms and legs.

Audiometrician reports a certain loss of hearing.

Joan is very happy and adjusted in school. Although she never initiates any new activity, she often joins in on the fringe of things.

Enjoys singing – voice quite tuneless. Plays the glockenspiel quite gently but haphazardly having no real idea of how many times she must hit to make one sound. Has a go every time she goes by.

Has started taking small things home from school. A tiny scent bottle missing from a display table today. Joan had it but Betty returned it the next day. These things are always returned.

Lethargic this week, obviously not well.

Is now making squiggles under my writing in her book.

Absent for three days with a chesty cold. Not really well on return. Absent for three days. Still has a cough.

Summer term 1964

A sudden interest in dressing up. Just stands around in dressing up clothes.

One to one correspondence not yet stable but can count to ten from memory. Has a certain success in 'matching' activities. Enjoys shopping play and shows a remarkable knowledge of names of coins and I think she is aware of their order in value as she knows which will purchase the most.

Enjoyed the festivities of Open Day tremendously and very obviously loves sand and water play.

Paints, but usually in one colour. A note from mother complaining that Joan must not paint if she is going to get it all over herself, 'It costs a lot of money to keep them dressed properly.'

I now make sure that Joan is well wrapped up in a shirt and rubber apron before she indulges in painting.

Trouble about taking dress off for PE, obviously selfconscious about torn and dirty underclothes. Provided her with two new sets of underclothes.

Glasses not worn – note to mother. Mother came up to see headteacher and was brought over to classroom to see Joan and me. Father out of work – free dinners arranged.

Copied her name and filled a page with her name written repeatedly – delighted.

Talks more and laughs freely. Seems happy and settled.

Is looking at books more but holds the book close up to her nose. Never sits to hear one of my stories. Usually plays in the Wendy House but occasionally I am aware of silence and Joan is listening intently to parts of the story.

Has spells of seemingly vacant daydreaming.

Makes up words as she reads.

A period of playing at 'being a dog' in house play.

Autumn term 1964

Joan opening up, talks more and is obviously beginning to look after her own cleanliness now. The humour is still very obvious and she has quite a mischievous glint in her eye. Watching often to see her effect on me or other children.

During a whole group story the other day she crept stealthily but obviously out of the house corner, tripped down the stairs, glanced back at me, stole over to the sand tray outside, poked in it, drove her arm in up to her elbow and danced off to the main building waving her arms in the air.

Joan loves music and sits enraptured whenever I play a record. Joan enjoys playing the drum or the cymbals when we are orchestrating songs and now realizes how to hit once or twice. More is confusing for her. She grins happily at every loud sound.

Joan certainly concentrates on everything she wants to do and puts herself into things body and soul. She is now mixing colours and spends a long time putting them on paper. She actually watches the paint closely as it goes on to the paper.

Joan ill in school today. I took her home. Mother seemed very concerned and we chatted about Joan.

Recently she has taken to dropping spots of colour into the sink and turning the tap on slightly to see the effect. This fascinates her for long periods of time.

Joan becoming more solitary. The other children do not take her into their activity very often now. She doesn't seem to mind this.

Got involved with filling jars with water and dropping colours in and then carried over to bubbles which she loved. She blew a mass of bubbles from a straw into a beaker and peered in saying: 'Look at all the little windows' (reflected separately in each bubble) and then added some paint to make coloured bubbles.

Joan started pretending to be a sleep walker today which fascinated the other children and they decided to do a play about a child who walked in his sleep and got lost. Joan was included but before long she was back saying: 'They won't let me be in it' and the children said: 'She won't do what she's supposed to do', and 'she doesn't understand' – sad.

Spring term 1965

Joan wanted to tell a story in storytime today and held the children's attention for about five minutes. It was about a robot who danced and she demonstrated by twisting and moving stiffly.

She was studying and handling a large stone chalk piece full of holes talking to herself: 'A little wriggly worm went in and there's a hole where a little mouse lives' as she poked her fingers into the holes.

Copies my writing now and loves to sit and listen to stories.

Enjoys 'message taking'.

Joan asked for a reading book of her own and I read one through to her. She thoroughly enjoyed this and when we had finished, closed it and took it to put it in her drawer.

Sharpened all the pencils with the pencil sharpener. Very proud and jealously guarded the job from encroachment by other children. I heard her say condescendingly to Dean, 'You can do one.' She laid them out very neatly with the big ones together and the little ones. I asked her to sort out the badly chewed ones which she did and Margaret helped her to count each group. She then took a message asking for twelve new pencils.

Can now dress herself and do all her buttons up but still has difficulty with shoe laces.

Still has no particular friend. Gets on very well with Carol, a new entrant and mothers her. Spends a lot of time alone but seems quite contented with her own company.

Summer term 1965

Joan has been making up songs recently. 'Listen,' she'll say, and then will go on with some long involved mixture of words to an 'up and down melody' and then she'll say: 'I can speak English.' I will reply: 'Oh let's hear some' and then she says a gibberish word. I say: 'What does that mean?' Joan giggles a lot and then says: 'He walked downstairs – O, I don't know!'

Still fascinated by sand and water – not even a glimmering of concept of conservation but fascinated by pouring and mixing. Uses sand imaginatively with toy animals and people.

After story today which she now listens to carefully, said: 'I love stories, I wish we had a hundred.'

Understands how to count things now.

Mother attended parents' interview. Most surprising – her first attendance at one of these functions.

Joan mature in her behaviour at the dinner table. Helps to serve.

Coming back after school with younger sister. Walks round and looks. Asks lots of questions, How? Why? Very excited about her transfer to the junior school. Has enjoyed all her visits and is already known and accepted there.

Transfer to junior school.

Autumn term 1965
In her first family grouped junior class she has settled down quite well. She is quiet and unobtrusive but is obviously excited at this new experience. Hangs on every word I say but does not always understand or remember.

Appears to be on the edge of activities and does not become actively involved. Enjoys watching the other children and does not appear to be embarrassed at playing a minor role. Often looks at me with a wide, understanding grin and seems to want my approval of everything she does.

Has learned to use the tape recorder and listens to recorded stories whenever she can. Only looks at the pictures in the book of the story to which she is listening.

Spring term 1966
Each morning has begun to confide in teacher with one short sentence 'My sister is married' or 'I am going to have tea with my sisters.'

Draws pictures and likes to tell me the story of the picture.

Speech does not improve much, referred to speech therapist for treatment. Therapist found it difficult to get her to talk at the first interview and asked her to name some objects in the room. To her surprise she replied: *'La fenêtre, la porte!'*

Today chose to work in the maths corner and has used pegs and pegboard. Can count up to 100 and up to 10 in twos.

Has begun staying behind after school for a few minutes to talk to the teachers.

Enjoys visiting the caravan with five other children from her class. Enjoys working with the tape recorder in the caravan. Always giggles when she hears her own voice played back and has found another friend in this teacher.

Summer term 1966
At her own request has begun to learn the descant recorder. Hasn't missed a practice so far and is making progress. Takes recorder home every evening. Mother says she is always practising at home.

Mother accepts gift of secondhand gaberdine macintosh, wellingtons and shoes for winter wear.

Joan absent for two weeks with a chesty cold.

Not long after her return from absence she lost her gloves – could not be found. I took her home in her car – she was tearful but enjoyed the experience. Gloves found at home. Long talk to mother who shows delight at Joan's happiness at school.

Given Deeside Intelligence Test today. IQ 78.

Interested in mathematics. Enjoys playing number games with other children and occasionally wins.

Now plays with the recorders once a week in morning assembly. Always the last to arrive, appears to play most of the notes in the more simple hymns.

Showing much more confidence, is smarter in appearance.

First day in the swimming pool. Joan does not possess a swimming cap or costume. Disappointment for Joan so secondhand ones obtained for her. Mother brings her to school today and asks me to look after her at swimming. Enjoys her first dip when in the pool. She looks thinner than the rest.

Autumn term 1966
Spent the day at Twycross Zoo, clung close to me and talked all the time. Very observant, showed special interest in the very young animals. Mother paid half the cost.

Member of recorder group which played at end of term musical evening.

Great improvement in speech. Still has speech therapy weekly.

New glasses improve her appearance. Patch on lens has been removed.

Has acquired a more relaxed and controlled attitude to 3R work. Mechanical reading age 6·5 years.

Takes charge of class shop and is able to give correct change.

Spring term 1967
Has sustained a friendship with seven-year-old Tina in her class for the last six months. Looks after her, fusses rather and is very possessive. Has a party for her ninth birthday. Tina is the only visitor.

Visited home with regard to free clothing issue. Home much improved. Mother says she is able to get on with the housework since the youngest started school. Back garden is now cultivated. Staff have been visiting home for the last ten years and none have ever met father.

Has transferred from ita to t o successfully.

Her stories are about Tina or about home. Fewer illustrations, more text.

Summer term 1967
Swam first few strokes today.

Dress and appearance much improved, mixed more freely with other children and has developed much more self confidence.

Plays the recorder well.

Talks to visitors freely when approached.

Visits caravan less and less. Teacher thought that to stop her visits suddenly might upset her.

Has developed an interest in picture making, for many months only produced designs.

Grade I swimming certificate. It has been decided that she will move to a third- and fourth-year vertically grouped class with the rest of her year.

Through her achievement in being able to read, swim and play the recorder, her powers of concentration and confidence are improving all the time. She still has no close friends but seems to be accepted by her classmates.

Autumn term 1967
Has settled in third- and fourth-year class.

Still enjoys her visits to the caravan; her reading ability has regressed since the end of last term.

Very proud of a dress she made for a puppet. The stitching was clumsy but the effect was pleasing.

The music teacher has kept her in the second-year recorder group. Her reading of music is poor and she usually learns a tune by heart.

For the first time mother is dressing her in suitable clothes for the winter without help.

Joan is excited and is telling everyone that she is an aunty and that her sister has had a baby. She can hardly wait to see it.

Gives correct change when helping in the shop.

Joins in group activities but is given only manual jobs by other children.

Today she has painted sheets of cardboard grey which have already been cut out for assembling as castle walls. She enjoys making a contribution in this way and learns a great deal from listening to other children's discussions.

Produced her greatest written effort so far, 'Michael's Christening' with a crayoned illustration of the vicar holding the baby at the font. Another illustration was of the christening cake. Has promised to bring the photographs for the teachers to see. Made the story into a booklet and hung it up for everyone to read.

Has joined the local Sunday School and is excited about attending for the first time.

Helping two other girls with a collage of a winter scene. Has brought some material from home.

In speech and writing is using longer and more complex sentence construction. Spelling is still poor but uses her personal dictionary often. General progress is slow. Enjoys grouping with pegs – groups of twos and fives.

Unable to persuade mother to allow Joan to join the group visiting Church Langton for an art and craft week although financial help was offered.

Still visits caravan mainly to choose another book and talk to the teacher.

Reading age 8·1 years.

Carol, a new girl who lives near Joan and is the same age, has joined the class. She is physically more mature than Joan but has learning difficulties and cannot read as well as she can. They come to school together and there are all the signs of a warm friendship developing. This will ease Joan's transfer to the high school.

Mother has attended both the recent interviews. Mother's personal appearance has improved greatly. Always sends a message when Joan is away with one of her colds.

Joan appears to be very much more self-assured and is developing a great deal of personal control but unfortunately does not confide in me so much. Is quite industrious on a shallow level but in most things she does, she is trying to please.

Will probably need extra help at the high school. Close contact with one teacher rather than with many specialist teachers would reinforce her feeling of security if this is possible.

CHARLES
Date of birth 12th February 1957, position in family 2/4

Summer term 1962
No outward show of distress at starting school. His mother was anxious to hurry away as soon as possible to get to work.

Charles is a big boy who seems vague and does not seem to listen to anything that is said. He makes no attempt to put on his own coat or change his shoes but just stands or sits and waits for someone to take over. Finds it very difficult to conform in any way.

Speech immature. A short-tongued lisp and uses baby talk.

Stood in front of me this afternoon holding his coat and shoes. Said: 'Me going home.' Always refers to himself as 'me'.

Holds his chin low on his chest and mumbles. Has a fantastic appetite. Awkward movements. Left handed. Nudges and pokes me to get my attention. Can be very irritating. Flat footed. Ungainly walk.

Charles is usually alone. He does not seem to have made any friends as yet. Suffers from catarrh.

If crossed or frustrated in any way has a sulky pouting face and withdraws from all activity or communication.

Brought his teddy bear to school today. He talked to it and about it all day long in baby talk.

The children tend to regard him as different. Christine and Robert were eager to look after Charles when he first came to school but he has been so truculent towards them, shrugging off their help, etc. that even they have given up with him. Relationship with other children is non-existent.

Joined in PE today without any obvious reluctance but was embarrassed.

Holds crayons in his fist. Poor hand control. Drawings careless and uncontrolled. Not really interested.

Never walks across a space if he can avoid it. Hangs on to walls or tables.

When I unlocked the veranda door today he said: 'What a lot of keys for one door.' This was the first real indication that he was at all in touch with what was going on in the classroom.

Talks 'at' other children in an absent-minded, vague way and seems unaware and unconcerned that they are often not listening. Tested for deafness. No loss, but audiometrician suggests ability may fluctuate with the severity of his catarrhal condition.

At parents' interview, mother said that Charles is quite capable of going home on his own, that he resented her meeting him each day and would I make sure he left school on time. This is an impossibility with Charles, he is always the last to leave and the last to arrive!

Charles doesn't seem to mind that he is not being met and surprisingly enough does arrive home.

Autumn term 1962

Has a lot of colds and ear trouble.

In discussion times has a tendency to shout everyone else down.

Plays aeroplanes at the break after school meal. He is so clumsy that his play is dangerous and as he blunders around he often knocks children over.

Beginning to show some signs of affection for other children.

Charles has given up his immaturity of speech. I have a feeling it was a defence.

Has started painting. Pictures are painted in a single colour, usually a dull brown or purple and very quickly executed in a few ill chosen daubs. He usually gives me a long dissertation on what the picture is about.

Spring term 1963

Reading through Charles's record so far, it does not show the many likeable traits which Charles definitely possesses. He is very kind. He is concerned if anyone is hurt or upset and gentle with the animals and smaller children.

His hamfistedness is largely due to physical immaturity in spite of his size. His hands are plump and dimpled and usually held curled with the thumbs hidden away.

He has shied away from painting recently and I think he might have been warned by his mother not to get paint on his clothes.

Has developed an irritating habit of saying: 'Daddy says it's right.' This when there is no comment by anyone to the contrary. Daddy seems to criticize Charles a great deal.

Charles still has a loud voice but doesn't shout down others in discussion quite so much.

Charles has a retentive memory and can recall in great detail something which has been done or said.

Mathematical ability outstandingly good.

He is lively and has an inquiring mind but has great difficulty in and diffidence towards recording anything.

I spent some time with him with the tape recorder today hoping that he would take to using it but he is not really keen.

His rabbit has produced six babies and Charles has been sufficiently excited to start to make a book about this.

Enjoys work on the large climbing apparatus and is agile. His flat feet seem to be the chief cause of his clumsiness.

Charles cooked today but got carried away with mixing and his soggy cakes did not get cooked.

Summer term 1963
After the holiday Charles was outspokenly rude about coming back to school.

He likes to assume an adult attitude and is very superior about certain things which he calls silly or babyish. At other times he seems immature and over dependent. He fluctuates between periods when he is full of nonsense and humorous jokes, puns and comments and other times when he is withdrawn and quiet.

Mother came to parents' interview and did nothing but run Charles down. She also made it clear that Charles's life at home is overlaid with anxiety because he cannot yet read the paper – 'Margaret could read the paper when she was six.' Margaret is Charles's older sister.

Talked to Charles about reading today and he said it is too much like hard work. Although I would prefer him to take things more slowly, if I can hurry him towards attaining more fluency, it might ease the home-engendered anxiety.

Autumn term 1963
When Charles talks to adults he could be misjudged as being cheeky but there is no intention of cheek. He does not seem to know how to approach people successfully.

Charles now writes legibly when he copies but his work is very untidy.

During the fireman's visit to school to service the fire extinguishers Charles followed him around asking incessant questions and ellicited some good information which I shall try to encourage him to follow up.

Charles much prefers to think out new things all the time and does not stay with one thing for long, although he has pursued the fireman interest longer than usual. He tends to do any written work as quickly as possible to get it finished.

Charles can always work out a way to solve a problem. The children who were running the hospital yesterday needed a stethoscope and Charles made one at home last night and brought it to school today.

Spells phonetically. Finds written expression extremely tedious.

When I asked who was six years of age Charles did not respond. 'You're six years of age.' He replied, 'I am just six, not six years of age.'

Charles has had a bad fall at home and is absent.

Returned after a week and is very restless. Is always asking if he can help. Goes round asking all the teachers if he can help them.

Charles is accepted by most of the children now and it is recognized that he can often come up with an ingenious suggestion or idea. He is the brains behind the space station construction which Andrew and David are actually carrying out.

Charles is intrigued by the books *Riddles* and *The Cat in the Hat*. He has already read them several times and delights in reading parts to other children. Reading well now and enjoys subtle humour.

Spring term 1964
Charles must make himself felt. He either gives demonstratively or alternatively pokes, grabs or annoys.

Earache today.

He behaved just as he used to when he first came to school. Very concerned that in a few months he will go to the junior school and he doesn't want to go. When I talked to him about it he said: 'You get pushed around in the juniors.' 'By whom?' 'By the other lads.' It might help if I encourage Charles to visit the junior school more often during the next couple of months.

Charles organized a circus, tickets to go in, performing animals and clowns. Very humorous.

Has started drawing lively pictures in pencil which are full of movement and action.

Contradictory again. Wrote a story today about a pirate and the illustrations were scrappy and hurried.

Charles's attention is directed towards only *one* thing at a time and in any one effort the peripheral things are neglected.

Just lately lots of his stories and pictures are concerned with death.

Interested in topical items of news. The rocket to the moon, etc and is pursuing information about volcanic eruptions and the origin of the earth. I have a feeling that father insists that these are the things he should be interested in although he does seem sincerely interested in this kind of information.

His background knowledge is impressive at times.

Constructed a 'factory' with connector and installed lighting with bulbs and batteries.

Absent with tonsillitis.

Returned to school. Concentrated for a long time on planning a motorway.

Is more involved with groups of children now.

A lot of information to offer and a wide background of general knowledge.

Brings press cuttings from home.

Summer term 1964
I asked Charles today when he last visited the junior school and he said quite seriously: 'I'm afraid I can't remember, my memory is not as good as it used to be.'

Worked out a game of chess on the 100 square board.

This afternoon Charles had a group of boys with him at the nature table and was giving a lecture on whelks. 'You see the sea whelk has air packs to keep it afloat on the surface of the water.'

He is quite often a lone wolf. Today he wandered in and immediately started to make crowns, swords and masks. He was quite annoyed when a crowd gathered but quickly adjusted and sorted out characters for a play about Richard I. He ignored the struggle for power within the group and just assumed that he was in charge. The children followed his leadership after a while.

When he left to move to the junior school he shook hands with me and all the other members of staff.

Transfer to junior school.

Autumn term 1964.
Charles is already known to many teachers in the school. He often brought messages across from the infant school and has a brother two years older than himself. He greeted his teacher by asking her if she had enjoyed her holiday and spent the first day looking around the room and asking questions. 'Can anyone take a book?' 'Can I take a book home?' 'What is this used for?' Any information he gained he discussed with any child who happened to be near. He singled the headmaster out at lunchtime and said; 'You've got the same car I see. Does it still go all right?'

A lost cat was brought into school by a child. Charles knew where it lived and promised to take it home.

Spring term 1965
Brought a 'cello to school and presented himself to the music teacher. Father had already taught him to play a few notes.

Has begun to work well in class. Enjoys painting and produces very colourful pictures.

He reads well and writes long, imaginative stories. Asks for help with spelling.

Organizes groups for number games. He is very quick and often wins.

When he has finished a piece of work he stands back to observe the activities in the room and talks very seriously to any child who goes near him. 'Have you been on those bulbs and batteries? What's it like?' Asked me; 'How old have you got to be to be in the football team?' His usual comment when he receives a reply is 'Oh!' as he walks off in deep thought.

Summer term 1965
Has become interested in spiders. Brought a web to school which he

had caught on a saucepan lid. Next day brought a large spider in a cardboard box and waited for it to weave a web. Read two books about spiders and is writing about different types of spiders and their webs. Has made a large web out of milk straws.

Enjoys working with clay and keeps himself remarkably clean for Charles. Has made an ashtray for his father which I have promised to fire.

He is by turns gregarious and isolated.

Always seems to know what he is going to do the moment he arrives in the classroom.

Reads frequently and often stops to observe the other children over the top of his book.

Making good progress on the 'cello.

Has not become involved in any spontaneous drama.

Very good at PE and swims well.

Autumn term 1965
Enjoys Carl Orff music. Composes complex rhythms on the xylophone. Can repeat a rhythm using the same notes a week later.

Always turns up on Saturday mornings to school football matches wearing football boots and joins in the preliminary kick about.

I suspect there may be a tendency to epilepsy. Sometimes Charles is lost in thought and I cannot immediately get through to him. Medical Department have promised to send a doctor to see him. I asked mother if Charles daydreams at home. She said she had noticed this but accepted it as part of his personality. Doctor will keep Charles under observation. Not necessary to give him any tests unless there is a significant change in his behaviour.

Spring term 1966
Charles is interested in any school visit and is observant. Was lost in the museum. When found, quite oblivious of the fact that he was alone or had caused any inconvenience.

Works well and quickly in maths but only for short periods. Progressing well.

Enjoys anything involving science. Engaged in experiments on sound. Insisted on complete silence for the testing of a telephone which he has made. Worked this up to a dramatic situation.

A group arrangement of natural objects they have found.

Two girls improvising a play with the puppet theatre.

Summer term 1966
Thrilled to join the school junior orchestra. Sits by the side of his sister who plays the violin. Can foresee a clash of loyalties when the time arrives for him to attend county orchestra practices on Saturday mornings, football versus orchestra.

As a second year child Charles is asserting himself as a leader. Younger children refer to him for information and help. His air of importance is increasing. Waits for other teachers outside the staffroom. Engages them in conversation at every opportunity. Charles is a staffroom joke.

Enters orchestra or string practices with the teacher, walks to his place, takes out his music and raises his bow indicating, it seems, that the practice can commence.

In the playground mixes with the older groups. When playing conkers or marbles every shot is vital to Charles. He attracts spectators and works up a dramatic atmosphere.

Sometimes he works with real inspiration and shows flashes of genius.

Has a keen sense of humour and is consciously trying to use a more subtle humour.

Autumn term 1966
Never stays away but often attends school looking quite ill. No further developments about the suspected epilepsy.

Some involved work with equilateral triangles and polyhedra. Accurate, well constructed models displayed with well written explanations.

Charles looking forward to next year when he will be in a man's class.

Charles needs a lot of understanding. His presumptuous, bumptious manner could easily be misunderstood. He takes liberties and presumes an acceptance of his mature standards which are unusual for a child of his age. Settles down well. Gravitates towards the older children. Has joined Junior County Orchestra. Persuaded by mother to drop the idea of football on Saturday mornings.

Spring term 1967
Has been chosen to be the class reporter for the school weekly newspaper. Interviewed new teachers for their impression of the school!

Joined in drama today but did not seem to enjoy it.

Charles disagreed violently with the statement made in discussion that human beings are as tall as their measurement from finger-tips to finger-tips when arms are stretched out sideways. To prove his point he is taking measurements of children and adults in the school.

Taking the part of a wise man in the nativity play. Dignified movement.

Meets me each morning and helps me to carry books and equipment to the classroom.

Summer term 1967

Has become fascinated with topic blocks.

Accompanies his thinking verbally for all to hear.

Class visit to York. Charles took some excellent photographs with a box camera.

Chosen to study Roman roads and is making a cross section of a road similar to the one he saw in the museum. Is jealously guarding an OS map of Roman roads and towns ready for this next part of his work.

Has decided to spend the first week of his summer holiday on a residential music course for the County Junior Orchestra in a Leicestershire school.

Enjoys French but is not particularly gifted. Accompanies the singing of French songs on the 'cello. Has now joined the French club.

Autumn term 1967

Brought note from mother asking if Charles could have a front seat in the bus as he suffers from travel sickness. I am rather suspicious. Not observed this before when travelling. Visit to Malham. Charles is particularly untidy with regard to his bedspace. He is always the first to be asleep at night.

Found specimens of wild plants which others have not discovered and has produced an excellent pencil sketch of the local church.

His rare personality and character are having a good effect on the school and his unusual manner is accepted with good humour.

DOREEN

Date of birth 3rd July 1959, position in family 3/3.

Autumn term 1964
Doreen was very fretful at leaving her mummy. Mother stayed with her in the classroom for some time. Mother had not brought her in to school last term for any visits. Doreen makes no response to my overtures of friendship nor to those from other children. She turns away from any contact. Sucks her thumb, forefinger curled round her nose.

I watched her come up the drive this morning clinging desperately to her mother's hand and drawing herself in from the other children as they ran by. Still very weepy. Settles until lunchtime when she is really distressed. Settles again until home time and then weeps.

Have tried to get her friendly with Diane and they do seem to do some things together now. Doreen moves restlessly from one activity to another.

One surprising move is that before storytime she brings a chair and puts it next to mine to reserve the place by me for herself. If anyone else sits there she sobs loudly. The children now bring the chair for her and this is her reserved position. Although her chair is so close she turns away her head and will not look at me or really join in.

Doreen is more settled now until lunchtime arrives and then her anxieties take control. Complains of stomachache. Really, just needs her mother. Mother is shy, timid and tired-looking but has agreed to have Doreen home for lunch to try to improve the situation. Things greatly improved.

Doreen is still very quiet and shy and finds it difficult to talk to people. She and Diane are now great friends. Often she has something to say to me but when she starts either she says she has forgotten or just can't get out what she wanted to say.

Spring term 1965
Is beginning to smile more but always holds her head slightly to one side.

Pencil control poor.

In the hall she stands around in bewilderment and is terrified of the climbing apparatus. Goes up and down steps bringing both feet to the same step each time and clings on to the banister rail. Where there is no rail, she must hold someone's hand.

Doreen is round shouldered, has thin arms and legs. She stands as

115

if she is fending off the outside world but occasionally gives a fleeting smile. She still has only one friend, Diane.

PE and movement lessons are a great trial.

Chatters a bit more now but still reserved and timid. She is overshadowed and protected by Diane but I think the friendship is good for her.

Left handed. Confused about left to right movement of writing.

Summer term 1965
Is terrified of dogs. Screamed with terror when one came into the school today.

Fearful of messy activities.

Dental inspection today. Doreen doing her best to be last. In the end she was coaxed into seeing the dentist. Makes a great fuss if only slightly hurt.

Doreen is trying to be friendly with the other children and enjoys being included in a group now. She is however often left out.

She enjoys the playhouse corner because she is always included there.

Stomachache again.

Told me that mummy was crying when she came to school today. A disturbed home background. Mother's anxieties seem to trouble Doreen terribly.

Models, drawing, painting, writing all very tiny and small.

At parents' interview learned that Doreen is afraid of the dark and has a night light all night.

Not interested in books. Looks at them briefly and puts them down.

Doreen needs constant reassurance and security. I give her a great deal of attention. She is so easily upset and defeated. Stands and dreams and only rarely smiles.

Likes to copywrite from a book.

Autumn term 1965
Paints easily now but always neat little houses or patterns.

Enjoys games such as snakes and ladders.

Draws people with enormous ears.

Doreen always seems to expect reward or punishment. Everything she does has to be seen and she will await anxiously for a judgement although she must know by now that she will not be judged.

Made an apron in sewing.

Painted a picture of her father wearing Air Force uniform.

Is obsessed with the fear of bogies and tramps and about someone who takes little girls away. Has an 'old wives'' way of talking about such things, nodding her head about it all with wide and frightened eyes.

She is often surprisingly forthcoming. Today, when a milk bottle was smashed and I went to clean it up, Doreen appeared before me offering the dustpan and brush.

Enjoys singing lessons.

Rarely indulges in anything spontaneously.

She has suddenly taken to woodwork and at this appears at her most uninhibited.

Mother reports that she is now much less shy and will mix with other children at home.

Spring term 1966
She refuses to stay at home when she is really ill and after laryngitis has come back without being fully recovered.

No tears at all this term.

Is developing an attractive writing style but written expression is static and usually involves mother, houses and children. Doreen frowns and screws up her face when concentrating. She holds her head on one side when writing with the tip of her tongue just protruding at the edge of her mouth.

Sucks her thumb less frequently.

Doreen rarely asks questions and seems to accept things without any further questioning or explanation.

She is passive and often asks to be told what to do.

Has been taught to do sums at home and enjoys doing pages of these but has little understanding of what is really involved. She counts up on tense little fingers pushed into her mouth one by one. It is difficult to get her interested in the wider aspects of mathematics. She is afraid to venture. Her reading too is mainly mechanical. She laboriously plods through the words with little real enjoyment or understanding. She must get satisfaction from it because she continues with dogged determination.

Summer term 1966
Although Doreen still does not like anything new she is gaining more confidence. Will not use the tape recorder but I have encouraged her to use the telephone.

Today she made a ship out of large boxes. This is a new departure. At last she seems to be opening out. Was also less inhibited on the climbing apparatus.

When she goes into the house corner now, she often takes over and can be bossy.

Doreen has been visiting the junior school regularly with Diane but would not go alone. She has already formed a *rapport* with a teacher there who knew her elder brother and knowing the family, realizes Doreen's difficulties. It would be ideal if she could go into this group on transfer. Diane is still her prop and as Diane is not suffering from the friendship it would be better if they could stay together.

Transfer to junior school.

Autumn term 1966
'I think Doreen will be all right,' was the remark made by her teacher after the first morning session. On the recommendation of the infant school she was placed with Diane her friend and in my class because I know the family. She is a worried, timid-looking little girl. She walks down steps one at a time holding on to the banister.

Arranged to see mother this week. Doreen apparently has been looking forward to coming to the junior school throughout the holiday. The last time I saw her mother was three years ago.
Spends most of her time painting and modelling in clay. Shows a sensitive use of colour. She paints people and objects without an outline. At close range the picture looks like a pattern or design but at a distance the picture takes shape. She seems to get deep satisfaction from her painting.

Talks to older children in the class but seldom ventures outside the classroom alone.

Spring term 1967
Her reading to me is rather slow and hesitant, lacking in confidence. Reads simple books in the reading corner quite quickly and can tell me about the story.

Mother says that bringing up the two older children has taxed her physical strength and she finds it hard work coping with Doreen who was an unexpected child. She could not understand Doreen's shyness and her emotional problems when the other two were so boisterous and strong. Seemed very happy that her daughter had settled so well.

Often gives the wrong answer in French but doesn't seem to mind.

Has joined the descant recorder beginners' class with Diane. Is the first in the class to bring a recorder bag made by her mother.

Staying at school for lunch. Normal behaviour in the dining room and in the playground.

Working with two other children at measuring. Can measure accurately.

Talks quite freely to other children and is losing her worried look. It is difficult to get her to write a story. When she does so it is short. Paints pictures which she talks about quite freely.

Enjoys music lessons, has a good sense of rhythm and concentrates throughout the lesson.

Today she took the part of mother in a puppet play. Her voice was clear and steady and characterization very real. Used many adult expressions and showed great kindness. This is the first time that Doreen has done anything like this and it is not surprising that this should be through the role of mother and from behind the protection of the puppet theatre.

Her movement in dance and PE is stiff and inhibited. Is always ready to help with arranging apparatus and putting it away.

Summer term 1967

Appears to enjoy maths and shows a sustained interest for long periods. Has collected birthday dates from children in the class and has discovered that most birthdays in the class are in May. Gone on to calendar work. Has calculated the days in a year. Discussion about leap year.

Doreen has shown keen interest in learning to play the recorder and has been helped by her brother who at one time learned to play too.

She has lost most of her shyness now and uses all the facilities of the school as freely as the other children.

This has been a good year for Doreen. Made many emotional and social adjustments. Very helpful in the class. Stays behind to help me tidy up.

Autumn term 1967
Plays a xylophone, glockenspiel or the timpani. Today attended her first orchestra practice as a member of the percussion group.

Slowly she has moved away from her preoccupation with home experiences and has become more adventurous. Today led an expedition into the school grounds looking for snails and snail shells. This was her idea and she collected the apparatus and books needed for this and arranged the exhibition afterwards.

Enjoys telling stories into the tape recorder and playing them back for younger children's enjoyment.

Mother finds life much easier and the family seems more settled and happier at home.

These five children, Pat, David, Joan, Charles and Doreen, have music as an element common to them all. The different home background, age and aptitude of each child, their physical, emotional and intellectual differences are accepted and each child is valued as a contributing member in the school. In the orchestra they play in harmony together and in the integrated day they are learning to live in harmony together.

CHAPTER EIGHT

Overcoming difficulties

It is not easy to discuss the problems of organizing the integrated day in general terms. Existing environmental conditions differ in every case and, in effecting the change, each school will obviously have different problems. Before changing to this type of programme it is essential that each individual teacher is at a stage where this represents a possible and not too difficult step in her own evolvement. If there are many on the staff who would find a great gulf between the integrated day and their present way of working, the approach must be very gradual. Teachers cannot change overnight. For the change to be sincere and effective it must develop through the teacher's own personal evolvement. There are many convinced and dedicated formal teachers who find that they can cope admirably when introduced to the integrated day. For example, in one junior school a teacher who had always worked with A stream children moved to take charge of an unstreamed, vertically grouped class. At first she was bewildered and came to the headmaster to ask: 'How can I teach something to forty children when they are at such different ability levels?' She was, in effect, recognizing that formal class lessons, even with A stream children, only reach a small section of the group, perhaps the middle group, which leaves the two extremes utterly bored and neglected. When it becomes necessary to think more deeply about children's development and the learning process and be more aware of children's individual differences and capabilities, a teacher cannot treat them as a class and will discover that she can more easily do the best for each child in the integrated day. There are certain children who are at a permanent disadvantage if they are expected to categorize, codify, classify and organize without having had the experience and background necessary for this. Many of these were in the past part of the 'C stream tail' but with the individual approach, their needs are now seen and provision is made for them.

The experienced teacher who can accept this philosophy and can provide an interesting and stimulating classroom environment may be satisfied with her first efforts but will soon become aware of the need to make day to day and even hour to hour adjustments. In one particular school, a teacher was eager to adopt this way of working and arranged her room in what seemed to be the most workable way. For a while, only a few minor adjustments were made such as extending the library corner to accommodate all the eager readers, moving reference books nearer to the construction table, putting the claywork somewhere more isolated where the attendant mess would not detract from the appearance of the rest of the room; but a general upheaval 'just happened' when the headteacher provided a water tank on a trolley as a piece of new equipment. Some children crowded round and were full of suggestions as to how it could be used. Some tadpoles which were in a goldfish bowl on the nature table were soon tipped into the trolley together with a few stones and more water and then the children wanted to go out on a pond-dipping expedition. When they returned with their specimens, the interest around the water trolley became so comprehensive, that the teacher was forced to rearrange the room to provide a larger working area and soon the room took on a completely new look with racks of test tubes, plastic trays, jars, etc. The important thing learned here was that the teacher must be prepared to make the environment adaptable to the demands of the children's interest and because this particular teacher was able to do this, their spontaneous interest developed and grew into a worthwhile study of pond life. There will of course, be some teachers who are unable to make any kind of adjustment towards this way of working and they would be well advised to consider a move to a school where the philosophy is more consistent with their own.

Teachers are vitally interested in learning about different methods of education and matters concerning the welfare of children. Staff are always eager to discuss and exchange ideas with their colleagues. Staffroom conversations often include the exchange of helpful advice. For example, one junior teacher was particularly worried about John who had apparently lost interest in his work and seemed apathetic and withdrawn. John had a brother Roy in an infant class and the infant teacher reported a sudden change in the pattern of his behaviour too. Roy had become boisterous and aggressive which was not in keeping with his previous character. Together the two teachers looked into the situation and discovered that the regression coincided with periods of time when their father was away working in Ireland and so the school was able to bring a greater understanding to bear on the situation. Again, a young teacher who was enthusiastic about working in this new way, was complaining about the continual spilling of water and paint in her room and from the suggestions of the rest of the staff, she was able to devise means which were more successful in alleviating this particular problem.

Teachers often become bored or dissatisfied after a period of teaching where they have employed a formal approach and begin to recognize that group or individual teaching may be more effective. From this thought perhaps even subconsciously, a new philosophy begins to emerge. If the teacher does not have basic sympathy with the child, understanding and recognition of his individual needs, respect for his dignity and awareness of his personality she will not be successful.

There is a danger in moving too quickly into the integrated situation without real understanding and thorough preparation. When all the barriers are first removed the teachers usually have an attack of insecurity. It is necessary for them to take a long objective look at the school and the children and feel assured that this anxiety is mostly self engendered. Once they gain a more relaxed attitude, forget their anxiety for a while and begin to watch the children there will be a gradual improvement and teaching will become challenging, interesting and exciting. In fact, the greatest problems are fears which come from within the teacher. External pressures which may be causing fear of criticism or fear of failure undermine the teacher's self reliance and she will need great determination to continue in the face of these. If the teacher has thoroughly understood the philosophy which lies behind the integrated day, she is able to interpret the principles with conviction.

When no timetable is provided by the head of the school, some teachers will feel insecure and find security in making their own programme for the day probably with the adverse effect of withdrawing children from some absorbing activity to work with the teacher. This shows that the teacher lacks understanding of just what is involved in the child's spontaneous learning. The children's own needs shown through their choice of activity are of paramount importance and this is the starting point for the teacher. Some of the children will at first be tentative about choosing their own work and ask frequently: 'What shall I do now?' At this stage, suggestions are necessary which will stimulate the children's imagination. The more timid child will perhaps copy another but again this is only the children who have previously been organized into work and as children come to work in this way from the beginning, these problems will not arise at all. There are also children who feel insecure if they are free to choose all day. Wide choice is too much of a challenge to them and some children will avoid anything needing effort. In the integrated situation, these attitudes must be recognized and provision made to deal with these problems. The insecure child, unable to choose can be helped if he is attached to a more assured child and the one who lacks effort helped to achieve easy success so that he will cooperate with the teacher as she helps him on to greater concentration.

In the free environment the introduction of too many new materials and ideas in a short space of time may lead to overstimulation and the children will react by becoming boisterous and overexcited or satiated and lethargic. With the new entrants to school this over stimulation is a common difficulty and it often becomes necessary to limit the activities available at first. Teachers can also be overenthusiastic to provide every possible type of experience for their class and the room could then become a mêlée of disorganization, overcrowded with materials and equipment and overstimulating for the children. Limiting is one of the disciplines which needs to be applied to the integrated day classroom. On the other hand, if not sufficiently stimulating, the integrated day can breed boredom and laziness in some children and these are very real dangers. Children who put all their energies into their work particularly the younger children, sometimes become exhausted before the afternoon session. It is important that the overall rhythm of the school should make allowances for the various rhythms of the individual children. One of the benefits of this way of working is that provision can be made for children to withdraw to more peaceful areas and less demanding situations when the need arises.

It may be a slow process for the teacher to become familiar with her new role, especially if a sudden change has been made from a completely teacher directed classroom. She must know the children really well and be aware of their individual personalities and needs. Much of the stimulation of thought comes from the classroom environment and can only be really effective if the books and materials cover as wide a range of interests as possible. The teacher must realize that the impact of the outside world may have little obvious effect on some children whilst it may inspire in others a flood of thoughts and ideas. Although direction should be avoided, the teacher must be aware when guidance is needed and be ready to make the right comment and ask the right questions. With encouragement the children will develop initiative and self reliance together with the free flow of thoughts and ideas.

Many teachers ask; 'But how do we keep records?' Teachers may be used to keeping records of each child's work and progress but it is no longer necessary to plan actual lessons in advance. Care must be taken to see that the teacher does not spend more time recording and observing than in guiding and advising the children. It is essential however that the teachers do write up things which happen in the room as well as an individual record of each child and that these are records and not mere assessments. They should include every aspect of the child's development. The older children can be responsible for keeping a weekly record of the time they have spent on various activities and of the progress they are making. The teacher however needs to look at the child from a much broader viewpoint than this and will begin to realize that the child's growth and development, his powers of concentration, his attitudes to learning, personal relationships, social adjustment and emotional stability are all a part of the picture. Whenever there is a significant observation to make, this should be added to the record. It will also serve a very useful purpose if an account of the story of the development of the class as a whole is kept and of the effectiveness of the experiences provided by various materials. Records of individual children are inadequate unless they show evidence of the child's stage of development. We feel that this is best done in a descriptive style. The record should be full of anecdotes which tell more about the child than mere statements or value judgements.

Teachers must always be prepared for setbacks and disappointments and not allow their enthusiasms to suffer. In the early stages, a teacher may work hard and develop what she feels is a good *rapport* between herself and a child who comes from a difficult home background and may feel a certain pride in her success. She must not be disappointed or discouraged when the child regresses, but must try to discover the various situations which contribute to the change in attitude and do something constructive to improve matters.

The teacher in her role as substitute parent must assume responsibility for dealing with problems of behaviour. In a permissive atmosphere the responsibility for self control and self guidance in work is placed on the children. The teacher must support and help them to learn to carry this heavy responsibility. The bounds must be firmly established and the children will then not waste their time testing 'just how far they can go'; but any inconsistency of treatment on the teacher's part will have an undesirable effect. The teacher must know her children thoroughly to be aware of each child's reaction to being punished and be sensitive to its effect on a particular child. J. C. Flugel in *Man, Morals and Society* brings to our notice that punishment and frustration may cause regression in certain children and that there may be danger in that it will intensify the children's fears and anxieties connected with early traumatic experiences so making them more obedient. It may result in greater rebelliousness which in turn is held in check by the super ego and produces greater hate in the child. Punishment is less harmful where there is no regression, for the child will be freed from inward guilt but will react with greater outward rebellion and this is not the end effect required by the teacher. Perhaps the best approach would be to spend time talking and reasoning with the child, bringing him to terms with the problem and for him to make some form of reparation.

In a changeover, the school will always go through a noisy phase. Too much noise or excessive quietness are equally questionable but as the children become more absorbed in their activities and learn to cope with freedom, the noise level decreases. The children need to realize that others may be disturbed by too much noise. Good manners are often thought of as old fashioned but this is one attribute of the previous formal situation which we feel should be part of the new atmosphere. The children should be encouraged to consider their effect on others and learn to prevent giving offence to them. We would be failing in our social education if they were not made aware of the needs of other people.

The formal classroom organization will have to be changed. It will need a great deal of thought to decide how to arrange the furniture in order to accommodate all the activities. The rooms must be divided off into smaller work areas. If the teachers are able to accept the challenge of finding ways and means to cope with the difficulties, they will be enthusiastic about devising ingenious ways of arranging and storing materials so that they are available to the children at all times. When the classroom has been rearranged there will only be actual places available for about two-thirds of the class, and here a brief problem arises when there is no longer a place for every child. At first, the children may ask: 'Which is my place?' but as new children come into the school, they will adopt the prevailing practice and this question will not occur. The ideal is for each child to have a drawer or locker but in lieu of this somewhere of their very own to keep personal books and treasures is necessary. In considering the practical implications of the classroom becoming a workshop, there may be many problems which at first seem insurmountable. The provision of room dividers, the geography of the room itself, the furniture, the possible lack of basic requirements such as a sink and water and access to the open air, must be considered. Improvisation may be necessary, particularly in an old building. The children's desks may be of the old type which are difficult to put together to make a flat surface. The blackboard and easel could be modified by being cut down and made into a painting easel which would be far more useful and give more floor space. The pinboarding and pegboarding on the walls may be insufficient and only one single section of wall blackboard is really necessary. If the head and the staff are prepared to think round even a very difficult situation with regard to organization of space and furniture, some ingenious and interesting modifications will be produced. These are often more effective than facilities provided by a new building. An abundant supply of fiction and reference books is required and they must be arranged so that they are easily accessible to the children. This system cannot work without books.

When some of the children are working creatively all day, the provision of sufficient materials becomes a problem and a large amount of wood and paint and other materials is used. There is also a tendency for the room to become cluttered and untidy. It is useful for the teacher to try to look at her own room occasionally as objectively as possible and to see how the appearance could be improved. The children must be responsible for clearing up after themselves and sharing in the general care of the room. The teacher's table tends to become a general dumping ground and this can be remedied if the table is utilized as a large working surface. Alternatively of course, if the teacher is over fussy about cleanliness and tidiness, the children are inhibited in their creative work and are never really able to lose themselves in any interest. If a communal space is provided where children from all classes can come together at various times of the day and use the activities, teachers will feel worried that they cannot see what the children are doing and it may take some time to prove to them that children can 'learn when the teacher is not around'.

When the teachers can no longer follow a scheme of work, they may feel insecure and unsure and as one teacher said: 'I wonder if I am doing the best for the children, it seems so nebulous.' There is obviously the need for some sort of guidance about general aims and about the stages of child development. In addition, a file of notes made up of things which are interesting and useful and containing lots of ideas which can be used to extend the children's activities will be a great help. The teachers will be happier and more secure once this has been provided and their work will be more effective. As the integrated situation develops, the philosophy of each particular school will change and grow with the school.

In some schools, the service time has been moved from nine o'clock in the morning to perhaps 11.15 or some other time in the day and the children are free to come into school and start work as they arrive, knowing that they will have a long period of uninterrupted work. At the same time playtimes have been abandoned. In one particular school this was done for a trial period of two weeks and at the end of the time no one wanted to return to the general upheaval of the traditional playtimes and the playground duties of shoe changing, first aid and yard duty. At first, as the school was naturally split into three sections, one teacher was on duty whilst the others had a ten-minute break for coffee in the staffroom but this did not seem to work. Some teachers were not ready to leave their classrooms at a set time, and, after trying various other arrangements, they found that the most workable one was to have coffee available from 10 a.m. to 11 a.m. and that each teacher had a short break at some time during this period. Now, at some point when the children are really absorbed in their work, the teacher goes for her coffee and her absence is almost unnoticed. The children are always aware that the teacher in the next room is available if needed in any emergency. The children have a self discipline and a commitment to the task in hand which is

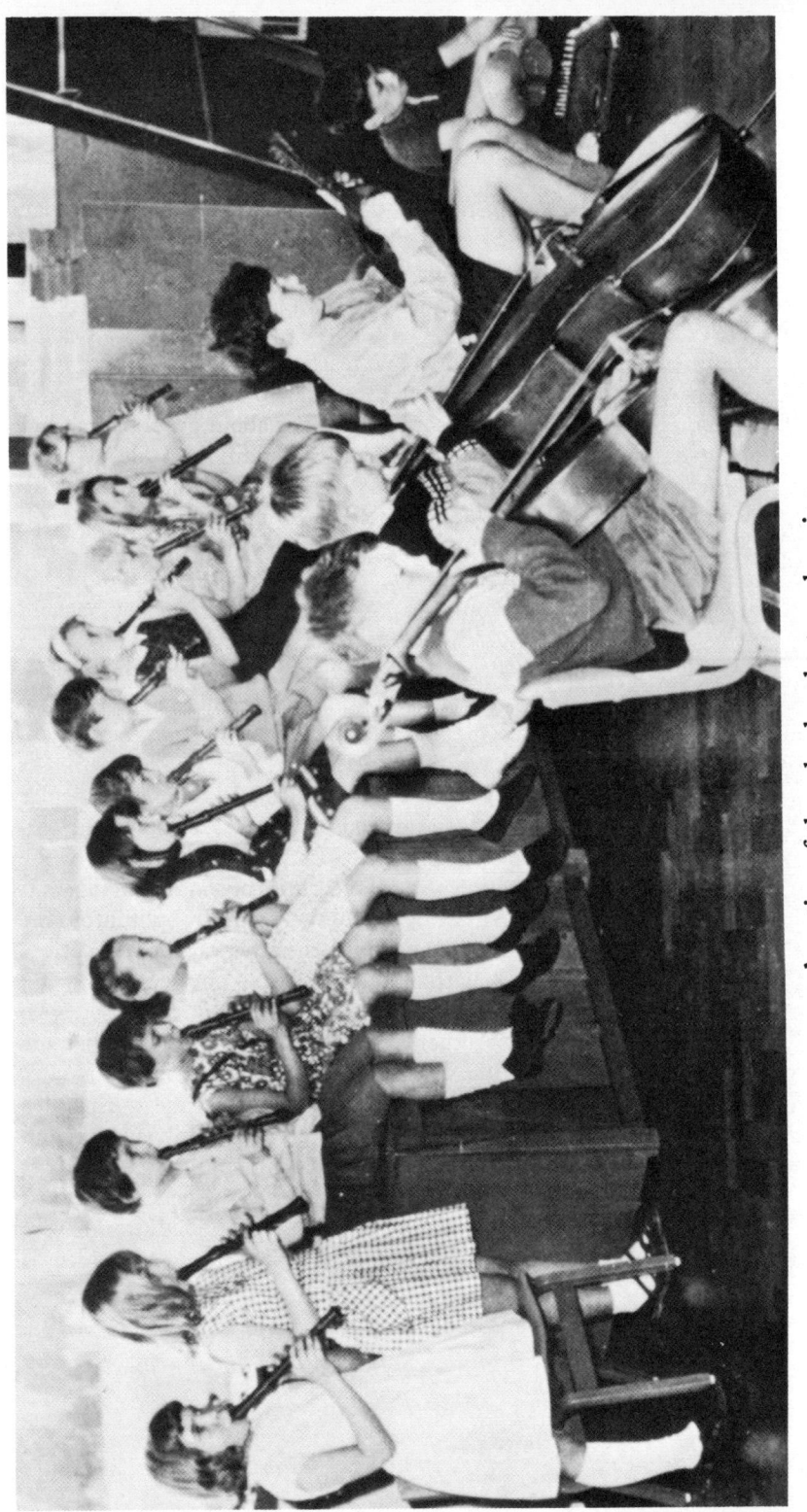

A section of the school orchestra rehearsing.

An impromptu drama group using clothes from the dressing-up box which has a place in every room.

independent of the presence of the teacher and they can carry on for this short period of her absence. This absence would have the opposite effect in the more formal situation where the teacher would be controlling the learning and the behaviour by her authority.

Although the classroom day is not timetabled, in the global organization of the school a timetable will perhaps be necessary for the use of the hall, for physical education, music, dance and dramatic work. Definite organization for the use of equipment such as tape-recorders, the use of the cooker, teaching machines, calculating machines and any expensive equipment which cannot be duplicated is necessary and definite provision will need to be made for wireless and television programmes. The subjects for which specialist teachers are employed, must usually be timetabled, although ideally this again could be a matter of the child's own commitment.

Teachers who are about to embark on the integrated day will find the situation far more demanding than a formal one. If the classroom is to be a library and workshop with the children working individually at every type of activity, it is difficult to see where the teacher starts. The formal class of forty or more working under direction is peaceful and quiet. This is a very artificial, unnatural and sterile environment for children between the ages of five and eleven years, for it is almost impossible for the child under eleven to keep his thoughts to himself. Movement about the classroom, children talking over the noise of hammering and sawing is the order of the day, but after a while, this does not intrude upon the privacy of the individual mind. There will be a transitional period before the new way is really established when the hangover from the previous way of working causes many problems.

Interest and cooperation between the headteacher and the staff is vital when starting this venture. An understanding and sympathetic headteacher gives great encouragement to the school. Opportunities for discussing any aspect of this method of teaching with colleagues will be beneficial. The parents too must not be neglected. It would save many misunderstandings and misconceptions in the changeover if the parents were invited to a meeting and an explanation of the new learning situation could be given and the advantages explained. Parents do tend to find new methods confusing and any opportunity of trying to explain some of the things which are being done in schools should be welcomed. Talks to community groups such as Young

Wives, Townswomen's Guild groups, etc are usually very helpful. Various points do need to be explained to the parents. They should understand that the small child's motive for learning comes in the first place from his own innate impulse to achieve, to find out and to master his environment, and that this is the point from which educationists work. They will soon realize that when the natural energies and interests of children are utilized for their own learning, initiative, cooperation, concentration and a sense of responsibility are encouraged, and they will see that as the child thinks about all he does, plans, remembers, concentrates and becomes increasingly observant, he is experiencing true learning and this is all directly related to mental development. Parents do not need the educational psychologists to tell them that no two children are alike nor react in the same way. They are all aware of this and we often hear mothers say of a younger child: 'He is not a bit like his brother' and so they realize that the children need love and understanding and acceptance for themselves as individuals, that each is unique and so cannot be compared with another. Once they really understand this, they will no longer ask questions about class lessons. Again, it needs to be explained that fear, anxiety, repression and insecurity are all bogies which cause emotional blockages against learning and that the sad thing is that these things can be engendered in the child by adults who have the best of intentions for the child's welfare and that it does not take long for children to sense that parents are anxious about their progress. If this anxiety passes over to the child in reading, for example, he will take twice as long to learn to read.

A most important element to be explained to the parents is the relationship between child and teacher. It should be brought to their notice that a child's loyalties are soon divided by parents showing disapproval of school, or vice versa, with the result that the child begins to feel insecure. This is even more likely to occur in the free day – it is only too easy. David comes home from school, 'What did you do at school today?' 'I played with the blocks.' The parents say: 'Played! That's all you seem to do at school nowadays. What about work?' This play of the child is comparable to the work of the adult and is something through which they acquire a mastery over their environment. David could have mentioned a hundred and one things he had done at school that day. He is unaware of the label to attach to the various activities. Instead of saying: 'I played with the blocks,' he could have said: 'We constructed a castle. It had a drawbridge which worked on a pulley system. We looked up in the science books how to make it work. We made some clay soldiers and found information about the right costumes from a reference book. We painted some pictures and wrote stories about them. The castle was measured and a scale plan made and then the teacher gave us some books and questions with problems to be solved about it . . . and then . . . and then . . .' and it becomes clear to the parents that this play is very hard work. Our aim is to encourage children to work as well as possible using lots of apparatus, books and materials and as the children follow their interests, they are skilfully helped by the teacher. A fully integrated situation includes non-streaming and vertical or family grouping. This also needs to be explained to parents because they do not understand if the child stays in one class for two consecutive years, or if younger children are in a class with older children.

Difficulties arise if other schools in the area are not working this way and parents tend to question this. They often seem to approve a more formal approach because of their lack of knowledge and because of their own school experience. Parents also find it hard to understand that the child can be learning if he is happy and enjoying school. They sometimes seem to think that school should be an unpleasant experience as it was for many of them. Many parents are at first worried by the apparent lack of competition in this system when they think ahead to the highly competitive values of the adult world in our society. There is competition but each child is competing to reach a higher level of aspiration for himself alone. In the higher age ranges of the junior school, competition is introduced between groups such as houses or classes. Competition between individuals even at this stage needs to be handled wisely and opportunity provided for all to excel at something and not be restricted merely to academic attainment.

An integrated day will fail completely if the teacher does not provide a rich and stimulating environment. It will fail completely if she is not enthusiastic and spontaneous in her involvement with the children and the development of their activities.

A real problem exists if the local authority does not understand and cooperate in this reorganization of the school. If their help is available it is invaluable.

CHAPTER NINE

Postscript

In education there never can be an end and a satisfactory point of arrival. There must always be progress and although the schools described here are developing along progressive lines, they have not, in any sense of the word, arrived.

There are many teachers who have come to the realization that the best approach to learning is when the individual child is allowed choice and the opportunity of following his own interests. This has been something which teachers have developed in their classrooms through an intuitive awareness of the child's needs and practical application. It is often later that the teacher discovers that this is reinforced by evidence from recent educational research and investigation into child development and the learning process. The possibility for future development is strengthened with the recent educational philosophy as a framework. The philosophers and psychologists affect the teacher's work and this is reciprocal. The process is self perpetuating.

If we look at the school day as a whole, the period between morning and afternoon school is the time which is least in keeping with the general philosophy of education. A relaxed atmosphere pervades the school until lunchtime approaches and then school meals often seem to necessitate regimentation controlled by authority. After lunch the children are usually sent to play for as long as an hour on a barren overcrowded playground. A more natural way of conducting the meal could be devised if headteachers and staff were prepared to think round the subject. The ideal arrangement would probably be with the school day starting at 9 a.m. and finishing at 2.30 p.m. A snack meal could be available for all children and this they could have at any time of their choice between 11.30 a.m. and 1.30 p.m. This arrangement would be far more in keeping with the philosophy of the integrated day.

The 'All Change' session, described in the infant school chapter, could be extended, so that each room in the school had the equipment and apparatus applicable to special areas of learning. With certain reservations, the children would be as free to work for as long as they chose in any particular room. For this to be successful, careful watch would need to be kept on each child, his work and his progress. This would probably best be done by having a couple of sessions each week in the home room with the child's personal teacher. It would not be necessary for the staff to be specialists and they would benefit from changing their focus occasionally to another 'bias' in another room. The interval of time spent in any one room by teachers would need to be discussed. The rooms would cover different subjects such as mathematics, science or English language experience. There would be a music room, a creative activities room and a general interests room. The children would move freely between the rooms following an interest through several subject areas as they do now and there would be no attempt to isolate experience into any one sphere.

The ideal building in which this might function would be the open plan design, where classroom walls do not exist but instead areas are devoted to different types of apparatus and equipment. Children could still be attached to a personal teacher who would meet them as a group periodically. This might take place successfully in home bays which could be extensions of the larger open plan area. Here too, the home group could mount any displays or exhibitions of their work.

It has been mentioned before that all types of material and apparatus need not necessarily be available in all rooms at all times. The school could have a central resource area for this where ideally, in addition to materials, the help of specialist teachers perhaps in maths, English, art, music or natural science could be available. The class teacher could request the help of the specialist staff in the classroom, refer children to them either individually or in groups and the resource staff would serve as a coalescent agent in the school. It is idealistic and beyond the bounds of possibility that schools could be staffed with sufficient teachers for this but a modification of this idea could probably exist in the form of resource areas equipped with specialized materials, equipment and apparatus. These facilities could even be shared by a group of schools in an area.

Education from five to eleven years in our two schools is divided into two parts. This has many disadvantages. Ideas for overcoming the problem of transfer from infant to junior stages might include the forming of a vertically grouped class of oldest infants and first-year junior children. This would bridge the gap adequately but a more realistic approach might be to transfer children at any point of time during a two-year period. The readiness would not rest on the level of attainment only but on the overall maturity of the child.

Schools covering the five- to seven-year age group tend to be staffed by women and there seems to be evidence that children miss the influence of men teachers during this stage of their education. Men should be encouraged to teach infant age children. To have direct classroom experience with infant children, would of course be an advantage for those considering the headships of all-through primary schools. This would, in the end, result in better understanding throughout the primary school, be an aid towards integration, as well as helping to provide a far more natural situation for the child.

The whole community is morally responsible for the education of its children and one of the aims of education is towards the further integration of the school and the community. Here, attention needs to be given to the three main groups of influence in the child's life, home, school and social environment. School can function for the child as the compensatory balance for any shortcomings of the home and the environment. For this to be effective, the teachers should feel that they belong and are part of the community and they will then understand the background of the children they teach.

The school must take the initiative if there is to be a closer integration between the home and community. School functions could be open to every member of the community instead of being limited to the parents of present pupils. Many of these people will be keen to identify themselves in various ways with the school and to help. Mothers of young children should be made particularly welcome and be encouraged to bring their pre-school age children up to school. In this way, school will be a familiar place both for the child and the parent when the child first attends.

Conviction about the necessity of involving the whole community in the life of the school will mean the school's adoption of the role of a cultural centre. Here evening centre classes, community college work, dramatic and musical presentations, art exhibitions, lectures and community group meetings would be held even in the daytime if accommodation were available.

The school's close cooperation with the parents and the home is vital to the well being of the child. It may not be essential to have a formal PTA as long as teachers are prepared to associate freely with parents in school and when necessary to visit them in their homes. A social worker appointed to a group of schools would help in this liaison.

Thought should be given to ways in which parents can be drawn more and more into the school situation. The school could have a social area where parents could meet for tea or coffee at any time during the day and gradually become accustomed to the school and feel at ease. The result can only be that of benefiting the children.

Future developments in primary education will involve greater integration, analysis and study, and as the fate of tomorrow's world will be in the hands of today's children, a tremendous responsibility rests with both teachers and parents.

APPENDIX A

The Leicestershire scene

Leicestershire is an extensive county and the homes of children attending Leicestershire schools range from those in mining communities, small industrial towns, urban developments to homes in villages and isolated hamlets. Most of the schools in these different areas share in the 'Leicestershire philosophy of education'.

These schools do not conform to any set pattern; they are not a copy of each other, but each has its own unique and individual personality. Each is a self governing community within the larger scheme of education. This has come about because the authority extends to the headteachers and they in turn to the staff both freedom and responsibility. In return, the authority receives loyalty, enthusiasm and cooperation from their teaching staff.

The climate of thought generated when a group of educationists value and use both the freedom and responsibility of individual autonomy, has produced a charged atmosphere where work with children is exciting and alive. It has created conditions where people are receptive to the exploration of new ideas, although a close scrutiny is maintained on the work which is being done in the schools, and what is more important, everyone is encouraged to question 'Why?'

Leicestershire is well known in the country for the early reorganization of secondary education which removed the responsibility for the eleven plus selection examination from primary school work. Although many infant and some junior schools had already begun to develop into places which were primarily child-centred, this removed the last barrier which had prevented some primary schools from taking up the challenge of providing an education for children up to eleven years of age, which was in keeping with their developmental needs.

Leicestershire Education Committee employs a body of professional advisory officers, whose function is to help and advise the schools. Tribute must be paid to both past and present members of the advisory staff, who, through their insight and vision, have had great influence on developments in Leicestershire primary schools. The role of the advisory officers is not that of inspectors. They are welcome visitors to schools and are appreciated for the positive and constructive contribution they make, as well as the friendliness and support they give to teachers and headteachers. They make themselves responsible for organizing courses, discussion groups and workshops of all kinds. They often talk to groups of parents and both introduce and encourage worthwhile innovation in various spheres of learning and school organization. Their attitude to schools is that they come as a working member of the team and work with the teachers and children on a practical level.

One member of the advisory staff is appointed solely to look after the welfare of teachers in their probationary year. These young teachers have his support over the first difficult period of teaching and he helps to iron out many difficulties. In the course of his duties, this member of the advisory staff holds group meetings for these teachers, where their particular problems can be discussed and ideas shared. Special courses are designed to help with the development of educational methods used in the schools. As a result of this, headteachers find that the young teachers are more effective and competent earlier in their careers than was previously so.

Members of the advisory staff also give their advice on the design and planning of new school buildings and school furniture and they in turn consult headteachers and teachers with regard to the practical implications. One feature of the newer Leicestershire schools is the care taken in siting the school to give as open and pleasing an aspect as possible. In common with the growing trend of improvement in school building architectural design and interior decoration are planned to be aesthetically pleasing and present high artistic standards.

The schools are however designed for children. By living and working in the pleasing and yet practical school environment, we hope that the children will develop an increased standard of aesthetic satisfaction and that they will carry this into adulthood. In most schools, original works of art by well known contemporary artists or sculptors are displayed alongside the work produced by the children. Original works of art are incorporated as a feature in the interior and exterior design of schools but they are also made available at regular exhibitions so that headteachers may purchase them for their schools.

Satisfactory personal relationships are considered to be of prime importance. The director, his deputy and assistant directors, the heads of departments, as well as officials and office staff, the education committee, school managers, headteachers and school staffs, both teaching and non-teaching, are keenly aware of the importance of maintaining this high standard of friendly cooperation. As a result, there is freedom of communication between all concerned in the educational sphere in Leicestershire.

In keeping with the general move, endorsed by the Plowden report, this is extended to include the parents of the children in our schools. They are frequently consulted and always informed of any organizational change at meetings called and addressed by the director or his deputy. All members of the educational system from the teacher to the director are available for discussion with parents should the need arise.

Schools within a certain locality dealing with the various ages of children meet regularly, so that it is possible to integrate the primary and secondary stages of education in any one area and the staff of primary schools can enjoy hearing something of their past pupils. The points of view of headteachers and teachers are discussed with the director at meetings held by him at regular intervals. Some of these meetings are held at residential centres owned by the authority and situated both within the county and in Wales.

These centres are in use during the year by groups of children of all ages for outdoor pursuits involving physical activities and field study work. Suitable areas are also being developed for the study of nature and wild life and for the children to be able to pursue such activities as sailing and canoeing. A remarkable number of schools in the county own or are building their own swimming pools. At present, plans are going ahead for the development of further local centres for teachers, where, as well as meeting socially, they can be involved in workshop situations, courses or discussions and have somewhere to make and test apparatus and equipment.

It is possible for all children in the county to learn to play an orchestral musical instrument at school. The available staff within the schools is augmented by the provision of specialist peripatetic teachers of music. All branches of music are pursued, but in addition, children can join the County School of Music which supports three first-class orchestras. Concerts are given all over the British Isles and Europe, a festival of music is produced each year. Leading composers are commissioned to write suitable works and at concerts and festivals great conductors are invited to conduct. Financially, the County School of Music is supported by patrons and by the organization 'The Friends of the County School of Music' as well as by grants from the Leicestershire County Council but they also obtain considerable income from performances.

There are various central facilities for schools such as a county library which loans books, musical scores, records and films and a central wardrobe from which schools can borrow costumes for their dramatic productions.

As in many other authorities the medical department makes available various specialists to visit schools. These include a dentist, audiometrician, doctor, welfare nurse, speech therapist, psychologist, social psychiatric consultant and a remedial teacher for the deaf. There is close liaison between these people and the schools and considerable attention is paid to the welfare of individual children. Headteachers are frequently invited to case conferences, which involve children and families connected with their schools.

There is close cooperation between the colleges of education and the schools. Each school plays an important role in the training of students from local colleges of education. The teachers regard this as a vital and essential part of their work. In turn, the colleges make many facilities available for teachers.

Much of the progress made in education is due to the quality of the individual teachers. In Leicestershire serving teachers are given every encouragement and financial backing to pursue all types of courses which lead to an improvement in their professional practice. New teachers are attracted to the county because of the obvious vitality of the educational system. Teachers feel secure when their Authority is always ready to support and help them and the schools and when it welcomes teachers with initiative.

This then is part of the background which has helped the swift evolution of educational progress in Leicestershire primary schools.

APPENDIX B

Suggested equipment and materials

FURNISHING

Working surfaces
Tables should be of the type which are easy to move and, if possible, stackable and with formica tops. Some tables with large working surfaces perhaps of the trestle type are useful.

A few table tops which are hinged to the wall and can be put up or down make useful work and display areas.

Tables for display.

Attractive occasional tables for book corners etc.

Benches with storage shelves underneath.

Raised platforms about 5 feet by 3 feet 6 inches and about one foot from the floor, again with an easily cleaned surface.

Various sizes of boxes or platform units for children to assemble their own raised areas.

Seating accommodation
Comfortable easy chairs/Wooden chairs/Cane chairs/Benches/Cushions/Rugs/Carpets.

Working areas
An area which can be completely blacked out possibly by using a screen and material.

Booths where children can work quietly and undisturbed.

Book corner fitments, standing units or book trolleys so that books may be displayed to show their front covers.

Three-sided screens which can be assembled for various uses and can be adjusted in height by fitting removable legs. These screens can be used for houses, shops, clinics etc.

Storage and display
Pin board areas on walls at the right height for children to use and if possible some of these areas should be covered or boarded so that children can work there and the pictures stay. This eliminates the selection of work for display. Easels hinged to the wall serve the same purpose.

Open lockers or locker units without doors and preferably with an individual small drawer for each child.

Fixed wall blackboard or double-sided easel-type board for children's use.

Some provision for storing dressing up clothes, bricks, junk materials etc, such as boxes, wire baskets, low cupboards or office bean stalks.

Vases for flowers.

LARGE EQUIPMENT
Aquarium
Book shelves
Cages for pets, birds and insects
Camera
Clock
Containers for water: transparent polythene on tubular legs/tin bath/rubber dinghy
Duplicating machine which children can use
Earphones
Electric cooker available for children's use
Kiln
Loom
Movie camera
Paper guillotines
Piano
Printing press
Projector and films, 8 mm and 16 mm
Racks
Reading laboratories
Reading master
Record player
Sewing machine
Slide projector
Tape recorders, transistor and mains
Tray to hold wet sand, preferably on castors
Tray to hold dry sand, preferably on castors
Trolleys
Typewriter for children's use
Various types of teaching machines and calculators.
Wardrobe for dressing up clothes
Wireless
Woodwork bench

ADVENTURE PLAYGROUND MATERIAL
Area of grass and trees
Area for digging
Barrels
Bicycle wheels

Big boxes
Felled trees
Growing trees
Ladders
Motor tyres
Old car with its petrol tank filled with sand
Orange boxes
Pramwheels
Seesaw
Sewage pipes
Slide
Tree trunks
Water supply

EQUIPMENT FOR PHYSICAL ACTIVITY
Balancing bar
Balls of all sizes
Bats
Bean bags
Boxes
Canes
Hoops
Jumping stands
Ladder
Mats, large and small
Plank
Poles
Quoits
Racquets
Ropes
Rope ladder
Shuttlecocks
Skittles
Storming board
Trapeze
Trestles
Vaulting horse

Window ladder

DOMESTIC CORNER EQUIPMENT
Bandages
Blanket
Bowl
Camp bed
Chairs
Clothes horse
Cupboard
Dolls, wooden, rubber and plastic
Dolls' clothes, washable
Domestic equipment for sweeping, polishing, dusting, scrubbing, washing, ironing and cooking
Kettle
Knives and forks, plastic
Pram
Table
Tea set, ordinary size, plastic
Teddy bear
Telephone
Towels

SUGGESTIONS FOR DRESSING UP CLOTHES
Aprons
Crowns
Doctor's coat
Fans
Glasses
Gloves
Hand mirror
Jewellery
Lengths of material for drapes and trains
Long mirror

Nurse's uniform
Policeman's uniform
Sailor's uniform
Shawls
Skirts
Stethoscope
Wings

COOKERY UTENSILS
Basins
Cake tins
Clock
Cook's measure
Egg whisk
Jelly mould
Measuring jugs
Measuring spoons
Oven glove
Palette knife
Patty tins
Pie dishes
Pinger
Recipes
Saucepans
Scales
Tea towel
Wooden spoon

MUSIC
Bells
Castanets
Chime bars
Cymbals
Glockenspiel
Home made instruments
Indian bells
Instruments from olden days
Instruments from other countries
Musical box

Orchestral instruments
Recorders
Records, classical and jazz
Tambourines
Tambours
Tubular bells
Tuning forks
Triangles
Xylophone
Zither

PUPPETS
Glove puppets
Marionettes
Ready made puppets for the children to use, and materials available if they wish to make their own
Puppet theatres, shadow, glove, marionette
Strong source of light

WOODWORK
Bamboo pieces
Balsa wood
Bradawl
Brushes
Corrugated brads
Cotton reels
Cuphooks
Dowelling
Drill
Eyelets
Files
Fretsaw
Glue
Hammers
Hessian pockets, fixed to a batten (to hold tools)

Hinges
Nails of all sizes
Offcuts of wood and peg board, all shapes and sizes
Paint and brushes
Panel pins
Pincers
Plane, simple surform type
Pliers
Ratchet brace
Sandpaper
Saws
Screwdriver
Screws of all sizes
Tenon saw
Twist drills
Varnish
Vice
Wheels

GARDENING EQUIPMENT
Cloches
Cold frames
Dibbler
Forks
Hoe
Lightweight roller
Line
Rake
Trowels
Spades
Watering can
Wheelbarrow

MATERIALS FOR CONSTRUCTIVE AND CREATIVE WORK AND INVESTIGATION
Abacus

Adding machine tape
Adhesives of all varieties
Aerators
Aluminium foil
Alabastine
Aprons
Arches
Atlas
Attribute blocks
Balance, standard
Balance with arm fitted with hooks
Balance with movable arm to vary length on either side of pivot point
Ball bearings
Balloons
Ballpoint pens
Balsa wood
Bandage
Basins
Bathroom scales
Batteries
Beans
Bellows
Bicycle
Bicycle pump
Binoculars
Bird table
Black paper
Blotting paper
Blue bag
Bolts
Books
Bottles, glass, polythene, squeezy, stoppered
Bottletops
Bowls

Boxes, all sizes from pill box to shoe box
Brick salt
Broom handles
Bubble pipes
Bubble rings
Buckets
Bulb holders
Bulbs
Bulldog clips
Buttons
Calendars
Calipers
Camera
Candles
Cane body clay
Carbon paper
Cardboard cones, as used in spinning mills
Cardboard tubes
Card of varying thicknesses
Cartons
Cellophane envelopes
Chain 22 yards long
Chalk
Charcoal
Chess sets
Chocolate wrappings
Clay bins
Clay tools
Clay trays
Clinical thermometer
Clock
Clock spring
Clothes brush
Clothes pegs
Cloves
Coarse sand – care must be taken to see that it does not contain lime
Cochineal
Coils
Coins
Colander
Collecting trays
Coloured pencils
Coloured ink
Colour factor structured apparatus
Colour filters
Compass
Concave mirrors
Cones
Conkers
Connector
Convex mirrors
Cooking oil
Cooking thermometer
Copthorne arch
Cork board
Corks
Corn
Corrugated card
Cotton reels
Cotton wool
Crayons
Cubes
Cuboid
Cuisenaire structural apparatus
Cylinders
Detergent
Dictionaries
Dienes AEM Material
Dienes MAB Material
Dog biscuits
Dominoes
Dowelling

Draughts set
Drinking straws
Dyes
Egg cartons
Egg timer
Elastic
Elastic bands
Elastic yarn
Electric bell
Electrical gear
Electric motor
Electrical wire
Embroidery silks
Equalizer
Expanded polystyrene, all sizes
Fablon
Fabrics
Feathers
Felt
Felt pens
Ferroplate mirrors
Fiddle frames
Filter papers
Flex
Florists' wire
Flour
Flower pots
Foam rubber
Food colouring
Football bladders
Frieze paper
Funnels
Fur
Gardening tools
Gauze
Geoboards
Geographical globe
Geometric shapes
Geometric shapes for filling

Glass beads
Gloving needles
Glycerine
Golf tees
Graph paper
Gravel
Greaseproof paper
Greyboard
Grouping sets
Gummed flint squares
Gyroscopes
Hardboard offcuts
H blocks
Health salts
Height measure
Hessian
Hex game
Home-made books
Hose pipe
Hundred square
Insect cages
Insulating tape
Iron filings
Jam jars
Jigsaw puzzles
Jugs
Junk boxes
Kaleidoscope
Kettle
Keys
Kitchen scales, spring
Kitchen scales with weights
Kite
Knitting pins
Lace
Laths
Lead shot
Leather
Leather offcuts

Leather punch
Lego
Lenses of all kinds
Lentils
Line
Liquid measures
Locks
Logic blocks
Logs
Loofahs
Madison project cards
Magnetic board
Magnets of all sizes and shapes
Magnet wire
Magnifiers, all types
Magnifying glasses
Maps
Marbles
Matador
Materials for mosaics
Material, man made and natural fibres
Mechanical egg whisk
Mechanical junk
Medicine droppers
Metals, all kinds and weights
Meteorological equipment
Methylated spirit burner
Metronome
Microscope
Micrometer
Minerals
Mirrors of all types
Modelling tools
Morse key
Mosaic shapes
Moulds
Mustard
Nail brush

Needles with wooden handles
Needlework paper
Net
Newspaper
Nightlights
Nuts and bolts
Nylon line
Olive oil
Old clocks
Packing paper
Paint brushes
Paint diffusers
Painting paper
Palettes
Paper clips
Paper fasteners
Paper for books
Paper punch
Paraffin wax
Paste brushes
Pastels
Pattern paper
Patty tins
Peas
Pebbles
Peg board
Pencil sharpener
Pendulum frame
Pendulums
Pentominoes
Pets
Phrase strips
Pinger
Pins
Pipe cleaners
Planks
Plankton nets
Plaster of Paris
Plastic cake containers

Plasticine
Plastic Meccano
Plastic windmills
Plastitak
Plates
Playing cards
Plot of garden
Plot of rough ground
Poleidoblocs, coloured and plain
Polyfilla
Polymer paint
Polystyrene balls
Polythene bags, small
Polythene tubes
Poster paint
Potatoes
Powder paint
Pram wheels
Press studs
Printing ink
Prisms
Pulleys, double and single
Quoits
Red clay
Reference books with authentic pictures and information
Rheostats
Resin based paint
Ribbon
Rice
Rigid plastic tubing
Rock salt
Room thermometer
Rope
Rubber tubing
Safety pins
Salt
Sawdust
Scales

Scissors
Scrabble
Screwdrivers
Sealing wax
Seeds
Seesaw balance on a fulcrum
Sellotape
Sequins
Sewing cotton
Sewing needles
Shells
Silver sand
Skittles
Slides
Slinky
Snails
Snakes and ladders
Snap cards
Soap flakes
Soda
Soft iron U bends
Spinning tops
Spirit level
Sponges
Spools
Spoons, graded sizes
Sprayers
Spring balances
Springs
Squared paper
Stapler
Stern arithmetic apparatus
Stones
Stopwatch
Storybooks
Straight edge
Straight tubing
Straw
String

Sugar
Sugar paper
Switches
Table tennis balls
Tape
Tape measures
Table covering
Table salt
Teapot
Tea strainers
Ten-second timer
Terylene line
Test tube rack
Test tubes
Textured paper
Thick lead pencils
Think a dot
Thin lead pencils
Three-dimensional noughts and crosses
Timberlay
Timetables
Tin lids
Tins
Tissue paper, all colours
Toilet roll centres
Torches
Tower of Hanoi
Toys such as cars, animals, birds, furniture, utensils
Transistor radio
Transparent flexible tubing of various diameters
Transparent plastic hosepipe
Trays
Trundle wheels
Turntable
U-shaped tubing
Vacuum cleaner
Velvet
Vinegar
Vivarium
Wall paper
Wall paper sample books
Washers
Washing powder
Washing up liquid
Water containers
Watering can with different sized roses
Weights
Wheelbarrow
White plastic dishes
Wire
Wood
Wooden balls, various sizes
Wooden beads
Wooden spades
Wooden spoons
Wood files, round and triangular
Wood shavings
Wormery
X-Acto knife
X Blocks

149

Bibliography

BOWLBY, JOHN
Child Care and the Growth of Love
Penguin 1953

BOYCE, E. R.
Play in Infants' Schools
Methuen 1948

BREARLEY, MOLLY
Studies in Education
Evans 1963

BREARLEY, MOLLY and HITCHFIELD, E.
A Teacher's Guide to Reading Piaget
Routledge 1966

BRUNER, J. S.
Studies in Cognitive Growth
Wiley 1966

BRUNER, J. S.
A Study of Thinking
Wiley 1962

CHURCHILL, EILEEN
Counting and Measuring in the Infants' School
Routledge 1961

CLEGG, A. B.
The Excitement of Writing
Chatto and Windus 1964

DOUGLAS, J. W. B.
The Home and the School
MacGibbon and Kee 1964; Panther 1967

Education Act 1944
HMSO

ERIKSON, E. H.
Childhood and Society
Hogarth Press 1964; Penguin 1965

EVANS, K. M.
Sociometry and Education
Routledge 1962

FLUGEL, J. C.
Man, Morals and Society
Duckworth 1945; Penguin 1962

GARDNER, D. E. M.
Experiment and Tradition in the Primary School
Methuen 1966

HOLT, JOHN
How Children Fail
Pitman 1965

HUNT, J. MCV.
Intelligence and Experience
Ronald Press 1961

INHELDER, B. and PIAGET, J.
Growth of Logical Thinking
Routledge 1958

ISAACS, NATHAN
The Growth of Understanding in the Young Child
Ward Lock Educational 1961

ISAACS, NATHAN
New Light on Children's Ideas of Number
Ward Lock Educational 1960

ISAACS, SUSAN
Intellectual Growth in Young Children
Routledge 1930

ISAACS, SUSAN
Social Development in Young Children
Routledge 1933

JACKSON, BRIAN
Streaming – An Education System in Miniature
Routledge 1964

JACKSON, BRIAN and MARSDEN, D.
Education and the Working Class
Penguin 1966

KRECH, D. and others
The Individual in Society
McGraw Hill 1963

LABAN, R.
The Mastery of Movement on the Stage
Macdonald and Evans 1950

LOVELL, K.
The Growth of Basic Mathematical and Scientific Concepts in Children
University of London Press 1961

LOWENFELD, M.
Play in Childhood
Gollancz 1935

MCKELLAR, P.
Imagination and Thinking
Cohen and West 1957

MASON, S. C.
The Leicestershire Experiment and Plan
Councils and Education Press 1963

MELLOR, EDNA
Education Through Experience in the Infant School Years
Blackwell 1950

NAVARRA, J. G.
Development of Scientific Concepts in a Young Child
Columbia University Press 1955

NEWSON, E. and J.
Patterns of Infant Care
Penguin 1965

PIAGET, J.
The Child's Concept of Geometry (1960)
The Child's Conception of Number (1965)
The Child's Construction of Reality (1955)
with BARBEL, I.
The Child's Conception of Space (1956)
Routledge

PIAGET, J.
Play, Dreams and Imitation in Childhood
Routledge 1962

PLOWDEN REPORT
Children and their Primary Schools
HMSO 1967

REDL, F.
Children Who Hate
Collier Macmillan 1965

REDL, F. and WINEMAN, DAVID
The Aggressive Child
Free Press 1957

RICHARDSON, ELWYN S.
In the Early World
New Zealand Council of Educational Research 1964

RIDGWAY, LORNA and LAWTON, IRENE
Family Grouping in the Primary School
Ward Lock Educational 1968

RIESMAN, DAVID
The Lonely Crowd
Yale University Press 1959

SCHONELL, F. J.
Backwardness in the Basic Subjects
Oliver and Boyd 1948

SEALEY, L. G. W. and GIBBON, V.
Communication and Learning in the Primary School
Blackwell 1963

SPROTT, W. J. H.
Human Groups
Penguin 1967

STURMEY, C. (ed)
Activity Methods for Children Under Eight
Evans 1950

TANNER, J. M.
Education and Physical Growth
University of London Press 1961

VALENTINE, C. W.
The Normal Child
Penguin 1967

VYGOTSKY, L. S.
Thought and Language
MIT Press 1965

Index

buildings, school   12, 15-17, 133, 137
child development   36-42
communication   59-60
community use of the school   134-5
creative work   61-62

discipline   26

Education Acts   11
experiments in education   11, 12

facilities in the classroom   21-24, 127, 134
French   78

in-service training   32
integrated day
   definition   12-13
   development   12-24
   environment for   15-24
   infant school   43-66
   junior school   67-79
   starting a scheme   121
intellectual development   58-59

language skills   58-59
Leicestershire Education Authority   136-9

mathematics   62-64
music   64, 77

newpaper, school   71, 75

organization of the day   46, 132-3

parents   34, 129-31, 134-5
personal relationships   58
physical education   64-65, 76
Piaget, J.   11, 29, 38
planning of rooms   127
puppetry   61

reading   60-61
records   125
religious education   64
room arrangements   18-21, 127

science   64
slow learners   77-78
social experience   58-59
starting school   17-18

teacher-child relationship   26-28
teacher's role   25-35
television   76
testing   32-33
timetabling   12-13, 62
transfer to junior school   67-68

vertical grouping   43-44
visits   72-73

157